AWAKENING TO UNCONDITIONAL LOVE

TRANSFORMATIONAL HEALING

BY DEBRA MITTLER

This book is dedicated to YOU.
May you come to know, experience and LOVE
the Beautiful, Divine Being you are.

Much LOVE and LIGHT to you on your journey.
Love,
Debra

Acknowledgments

With heartfelt love and gratitude;

To my parents Arnold and Barbara Mittler for your love, for providing for me and for being the perfect parents for me in this lifetime. I love you.

Thank you God, Spirit, Angels and all the divine beings who work with me, for your love, patience, guidance and presence in my life.

Thank you Ron and Mary Hulnick at the University of Santa Monica for giving me the tools to love and be at peace with myself and the world around me. A special thank you Ron for always reminding me to "Stay with and trust the process."

Thank you to all the many wonderful and inspiring spiritual leaders, teachers, authors and masters for sharing your Wisdom, knowledge and Love, I have so much gratitude for your contribution to the world and assisting me on my journey.

To my sisters, friends, mentors and clients, thank you for being here with me on my journey, your presence in my life is truly a gift.

Dear Reader,

Have you ever wondered why you think the way you think, act the way you act and feel the way you feel? This book came about from my desire to Love myself unconditionally, know who I truly am, why I'm here and what my divine purpose is.

In these pages I'm sharing with you a collection of my writings from over thousands of processes that have assisted me in aligning with the deeper truth within. By allowing myself to feel what I was feeling instead of pushing it down, ignoring it or numbing out and opening to my inner knowing, I've received profound wisdom, clarity, guidance and love assisting me in aligning with who I truly am; moving from just understanding the question or issue into the place where it transforms; ultimately experiencing wholeness and Unconditional Love.

It didn't happen overnight, however, over the past few years of doing this process my life has become more free flowing and peaceful, I feel self empowered and more in alignment with who I truly am, I feel Loved and supported by the Universe and I have a deep connection with God, Angels and all the Divine Beings who work with me; in "essence" I AM Living in the Loving.

Although these writings were addressed to me, they are not exclusively for me, nor are they meant to separate me in any way, I'm sharing them with you as an indication of what is possible for each of us as we find a unique connection to the Divine.

My hope in sharing my writings with you is that you find some recognition of your own path, you are guided to what is right for you, you begin to and continue to Love and accept yourself unconditionally and you give yourself the opportunity to experience the tremendous amount of Love, Wisdom and guidance that's already within you.

May you be Inspired, Uplifted and filled with Healing and Loving Energy.

Much Love,
Debra

What is Spiritual Healing?

We get to know ourselves through our experiences. Most of our brain functions outside conscious awareness and we often react to situations from prior "learned" experiences/memory. How we act/re-act and what we attract into our lives is usually determined by the information that's stored in our subconscious. Even if there are infinite possibilities in front of us, we habitually focus on those consistent with our earlier experiences; the thoughts, beliefs, perceptions and coping mechanisms that were created at a younger age. Most often we aren't aware of what's going on in our subconscious and we are blindly reacting from old thought patterns, some of which are still beneficial to our well being while others are not.

Our wounds or triggers aren't bad; they are showing us areas where we've disconnected from our source, narrowed our point of view and have identified with certain thoughts, feelings, beliefs and perceptions. These emotions are actually a gift; they are assisting us in becoming aware of the thoughts that aren't in alignment with who we truly are. By replacing judgments with compassion and Love, reframing misunderstandings, forgiving ourselves and others and updating our beliefs, our lives begin to flow more easily and naturally and we ultimately come into alignment with who we truly are. What may seem like a difficult situation in the moment often turns out to be a blessing, something that is assisting us in clearing memory/thought patterns that no longer serve us; allowing us to live as our true magnificence.

Since every behavior is motivated by a positive intention, when we acknowledge what we're feeling with compassion and love and we comfort the child within, a Healing and Loving integration naturally takes place, allowing us to experience Self Love and Inner Peace. Our inner being only knows love and when we are aligned with our inner being we feel Loved, Lovable and Loving and we easily and naturally begin to experience more Peace, Love, Joy and Happiness in all areas of our lives, in "Essence" we are Living in the Loving.

MY

WRITINGS

WHAT IS THE INTRODUCTION TO MY BOOK?

When you think about
Having an introduction, it's
A way for you
To
Introduce your writings and
Share how
This wisdom
Has come about through your own personal
Experience. By going within you've received wonderful
Insights, revelations and miracles; you've come to experience your
Natural self and the love of the divine. In noticing
The ways that you naturally respond without expecting things to be
Right or wrong, you've been able to
Open to a deeper truth within you.
Doing this process has helped you to
Understand the ways in which you were
Creating your life based on
The beliefs and perceptions you had at the unconscious level.
In becoming aware of them and removing the layers
Of judgments and misunderstandings, you've
Naturally experienced
The gentle
Opening of Love from within. By slowing down, opening your
Mind and connecting with the divine,
You've discovered fresh insights, new
Beginnings and Unconditional Love. You've now decided to
Offer your writings to inspire
Others to open to their own inner
Knowing.

WHAT IS TRANSFORMATIONAL HEALING?

Why you chose Transformational

Healing as your sub-title is because you've

Awakened to

The truth of who you are, and

In this truth you are feeling connected to

Source. Your book Awakening to Unconditional Love;

Transformational Healing is sharing your experience of

Reconnecting with the Love within you

And allowing this Loving energy to assist you in

Noticing ways to see and experience your

Situations from a more loving point of view.

Feeling connected to source has

Offered you the

Realization of how Loved and supported you are and it's

Made a significant difference in your life. You

Are now feeling Loved, Lovable and Loving and you're

Trusting

In yourself, God and the Universe. By being

Open to the

Newness of every moment, you've been

Able to experience a more peaceful and free flowing

Life. Transformational

Healing is the

Experience of

Aligning with the

Love

Inside and

Naturally flowing with the

Goodness of the universe.

WHAT WAS I BORN TO DO? LOVE?

Who am I really?

How do I achieve what I'm here to achieve?

Answers to your life unfold everyday when you

Take risks and step out of your comfort zone.

Whatever is buried deep inside you is

Asking you "When will you let me out?"

So when you're asking the question; "What was

I born to do?" think about the

Beauty and uniqueness that you already are. When you

Openly express your true essence instead of

Running or hiding you will

Notice how much you are in tune with your divine nature.

Today, take a risk, have fun, and enjoy all of your experiences.

Offer your authentic self in your relationships, it's not in your

Doing, it's in your being. When you

Open yourself more, more can express through you.

Live fully,

Open your heart

Venture into the world and

Embrace yourself and others with love.

WHAT IS THE MEANING OF LIFE?

What is it you really want to know?

How to find happiness and peace?

All your life you've looked outside yourself to

The material, not recognizing that the

"I AM" presence is what creates the meaning of life.

Situations don't create it,

True meaning is already within you.

Honor the divine being you are.

Enter into your heart and return to the

Magnificence of who you are.

Embrace yourself and your oneness with all

And watch the

Now become meaningful.

Infinite opportunities are here

Now, in the present moment.

Giving and receiving love is what brings meaning to life.

Opening yourself to the

Flow of love already inside you brings true meaning.

Let go, trust and surrender and

Invite the love that's inside of you to

Flow to everyone and everything and you will

Experience the meaning of life.

WHY AM I HERE ON EARTH, WHAT IS MY PURPOSE?

Why am I here, do I have a divine purpose?

Having this thought makes me wonder.

You do have

A divine purpose.

Much of your life you've felt

Insecure, not knowing

How to accomplish things.

Every time you start to fear, you

Return to self doubt and

Eventually become trapped.

Open yourself to the

Newness of this moment.

Every day is a new opportunity and today you are more

Aware and able to

Receive inner guidance.

Trust in your inner guidance,

Honor all of life and know that

What you do from pure love is what matters;

How you are experiencing and sharing Love is what matters.

Awareness of

This and putting it

Into action will

Soon

Move you in the direction of your divine purpose. In this moment say

YES to LOVE, YES to BEAUTY and YES to LIFE.

People, situations and money don't determine your purpose or happiness.

Understand that

Right now your

Purpose is to learn to love yourself and

Out of love for yourself, you'll be able to connect with others more easily by

Sharing the Love that you're feeling with

Everyone and everything.

DO YOU WANT TO EXPRESS THROUGH ME?

Do you have a plan for my life? I'm ready and

Open to hear you.

You are here to

Open and stretch yourself.

Understand that

What may seem scary in the moment,

Always turns out to be okay.

Notice what brings you joy.

Today, become more aware of what

Thoughts bring you peace.

Often things might seem to be

Extraordinary difficult, however it can be

Xactly what you need to learn and grow.

Place your mind on everything being okay

Right now.

Eventually you will be able to

See and experience the greatness of who you are.

Stay open to the possibilities

That are

Here now.

Remember that doors

Open when you are ready and willing. Don't

Underestimate the

Greatness of who you are now.

Have an openness and allow yourself to

Move into your life experiences

Expressing from/as the love and light of who you truly are.

WHAT CAN I DO FOR THE WORLD?

What you can do
Has to do with
Awakening.
To make a
Change in the world you need to be
Aware of what
Needs to change
Inside yourself,
Do that within yourself first and then
Offer it to the world.
For right now,
Open yourself to doing what's
Right so you can heal,
Then what will
Happen is the universe will create
Experiences
Where you can
Offer
Right
Livelihood and share your
Divine nature.

WHAT AM I HERE TO BRING TO THE WORLD?

When you

Have an

Awareness and

Trust that

All that you are

Makes a difference

In the world then you can appreciate that you don't

Have to do something

Exceptional in order to

Reach into peoples hearts, that you can be the

Experience of love and light everywhere you go.

Through your experiences

Opportunities to

Bless others with your presence will be

Rich and rewarding.

It's when you're living in the

Now instead of

Going into the future, you will experience

The

Opportunity to see all

That's

Here now. Rewarding

Experiences come

When you are living in gratitude and you're

Open to the

Realization of the

Love of the

Divine in you, as you and all around you.

WHAT DOES MAKING A DIFFERENCE MEAN?

Who am I and
How can I make
A difference?
Trust in your abilities and
Do what comes natural for you.
Other people are using their unique gifts,
Everyone has them.
Share authentically, that
Makes a difference.
Always remember you only
Know what you know.
Infinite intelligence gives you what you
Need when you need it.
Give yourself to this intelligence
And allow your experiences to unfold in
Divine order.
If you
Feel resistant it will stop the
Flow. Allow yourself to release the need for resistance and
Eventually you will see and
Remember why you came here.
Embrace where you are right
Now on your journey, you
Can't do it wrong.
Everyone is learning and growing.
Making a difference starts from within.
Embrace yourself and your life now
And eventually you will see that when you live from your divine
Nature, you are making a difference.

WHAT IS MY PURPOSE FOR BEING HERE?

Why you are
Here has to do with
Awakening
To what is
Inside of you, your
Spirit
Makes
You who you are. Your
Purpose is to
Understand and allow what wants to be
Revealed through you. Your
Purpose is to
Offer your
Spirit as your
Expression and to
Find
Opportunities to
Reveal the
Beauty and love that you are. Your unique
Expression
Is your purpose. Your
Natural
Giving is a way in which you
Honor what wants to be
Expressed through you. Your purpose is to
Reveal your natural self by allowing your spirit to
Express through you.

HOW CAN I BE GENTLE WITH MYSELF?

How can I be gentle with myself today?

Offer yourself compassion, love and understanding.

When you

Can come from

A place of compassion you're more able to

Naturally be gentle with yourself,

It starts from within.

Becoming gentle with yourself is the

Experience you get when you are

Giving yourself love, compassion and understanding.

Experiencing and expressing this is your divine

Nature.

Think about how good it feels to

Love others and when other people love you.

Embrace your own loving

Without judgment and

Invite the little one inside of you into

This loving.

Honor yourself and

Make love, compassion and understanding for

Yourself a priority.

Stay in the present moment and allow the

Experience of

Love to expand inside of you and

Flow into all of your experiences.

HOW CAN I TAKE CARE OF MYSELF TODAY?

Have
Options
Where you
Can be more
Alert to
Noticing what you need
In
The moment.
As you
Keep an open mind you will
Experience a way to
Care for yourself
And create
Right in the moment.
Every time you
Open
For
More insight
You are learning.
See
Every experience as
Letting you
Find a new way
To
Open to
Divine energy
And allow it to move through you and guide
You.

WHAT DOES LOVE MEAN?

What does real love mean?

Happiness and peace within and

Acceptance of all that is.

Trusting that all that you

Do and all that you are is perfect. Love is

Opening your heart and connecting with

Everyone and everything,

Seeing and experiencing Loving Oneness.

Love is an

Opportunity to be

Vulnerable and

Express your divine nature. Love is

Meeting each day with a childlike mind and

Embracing each moment fresh and new. Love is the

Awareness of your

Natural essence, Love is who you are.

How Can I Create The Experience of Love?

Here and now is an

Opportunity to bring to mind someone or something that

Warms your heart and

Choose to fill every cell

And fiber of your being with this feeling.

Notice how

In this moment you are

Creating a

Richness of the

Experience of love and

Allow yourself

To be present in this

Experience now.

This is

How to create loving

Experiences here and now; this is your true nature.

Even if your

Xperiences seem hard,

Place your loving into the

Experience and this will

Reward you with love

In each

Experience.

Notice when you

Create a block to the love

Experience and

Open yourself to the warmth of your heart and let love

Flow through your entire being. Coming from a place of

Love will

Offer you the feeling of love as you

Venture into the world and

Experience love for yourself, everyone and everything.

<u>*WHAT IS UNCONDITIONAL LOVE?*</u>

When you are loving unconditionally, you are
Honoring
All
That
Is and you are
Seeing with the eyes of your heart.
Unconditional love is
Noticing the
Care
Of the
Nature of the
Divine
In you,
Through you and all around you.
It is the
Offering of your true
Nature,
A natural way to
Live and
Love. Unconditional love
Offers
Value in everyone and
Every experience.

WHAT DO I WANT IN A LOVE RELATIONSHIP?

What is a loving relationship?

Happiness and freedom to be who you truly

Are and love, loving and acceptance are at

The root of your actions.

Deciding to love and accept yourself and

Others unconditionally

Increases your ability to be close.

What do you really want

And are you ready for it

Now? Know

That

In life

No one knows

All the answers, however you can have some ideas.

Letting yourself want to have a conscious loving relationship

Opens the doors to possibility.

Venture into life,

Embrace every experience

Right down to the littlest and

Enjoy each moment. Do you live in

Love now? Love for yourself

And all people?

Today, practice this first.

Invite the experience of love into your life daily and

Open yourself to the

Now moment allowing yourself to experience

Spirit's love flowing through you. Something wonderful is

Happening beyond what you can see right now.

I encourage you to be

Patient, relax, let go and embrace your Oneness with all of life.

HOW CAN I RELEASE THE CONFLICT?

Here is an
Opportunity
Where you
Can invent
A
New strategy
In which you are
Ready to
Experience
Love.
Examine
All that you
Say you want to
Experience about love
Then notice
How you feel.
Every feeling
Creates a flow
Or block/resistance. What
Needs examination would be the
Feeling that contracts,
Let this feeling show you what
It believes from past
Conditioning and then ask your higher self how
To resolve it.

WHAT ARE THE UNDERLYING BELIEFS?

Why you are

Having

A hard

Time moving into a love relationship is because you had

An experience of being hurt in the past and now you're

Resisting the

Experience.

The resistance

Has to do with the

Experience or experiences you had in the past.

Understanding why you think and act as you do is

Necessary in order to

Decide to have and

Embrace a new perception about a love

Relationship.

Look at how

You create a way

In which you feel you

Need to protect yourself.

Give that part of you a voice and notice the

Because's.

Expressing what you're feeling

Lets you know the reason

In which you fear or resist the

Experience now.

Facing it will help you

See the underlying beliefs.

WHAT CAN I BELIEVE ABOUT LOVE NOW?

What you can do first is
Have an offering of forgiveness
About
The ways in which you
Created a misunderstanding from past experiences
About love relationships and the idea that you
Needed to protect yourself and you weren't worthy of love.
In this moment you have an opportunity to create a new
Belief; that it is safe for you to
Express and experience love, that you deserve to
Love and be loved, you are made of love, it's your divine self.
Imagine what it would be like
Experiencing and expressing love easily and naturally.
Vision this with feeling, really
Experience what it would feel like in your body as you now
Allow it to
Become a reality in your life.
Offering yourself the opportunity to experience love creates an
Ultimate love relationship with yourself, god and others.
This new understanding of
Love will bring forth
Opportunities that will match your new vibration.
Value yourself sweetie, give yourself the gift of
Experiencing love. Allow yourself to experience your divine
Nature and the
Opportunity to enjoy sharing love
With yourself, others and your divine mate, you deserve it!

HOW CAN I LOVE MYSELF RIGHT NOW?

How you can love yourself is by

Offering a

Way that you

Can be more in

Alignment with your natural self. Your

Natural self

Is uniquely designed and is an important part of humanity.

Loving yourself is

Offering yourself the idea that you are

Valuable and worthy.

Expressing love to yourself

Means honoring the divine being

You are.

Saying to yourself "I love you" is one way to

Express

Love to yourself. Another way is allowing yourself to

Feel loved by

Re-connecting to the love

Inside of you and

Giving

Honor

To the star you are. In valuing yourself you'll

Naturally find love

Opening from

Within.

WHAT DOES IT MEAN TO BE NOURISHED?

When you are nourishing yourself you are
Honoring your body by eating healthy, drinking enough water
And resting. Nourishing yourself is allowing yourself
To have what you
Desire, it's
Offering yourself the
Experience of being
Sacred, loved and cared for;
It's loving yourself unconditionally and
Taking time to focus on you. Nourishing yourself is
Making room in your life to take care of your needs and
Experience what is important for you. It's valuing
And honoring yourself by allowing yourself to do what comes
Natural for you. Nourishing yourself is
Talking to yourself and
Others in loving ways and
Being kind and gentle with yourself in all that you
Experience.
Notice the ways in which you
Offer kind words and actions to others that you
Usually don't do for yourself?
Right now
Include this for your
Self. Nourishing yourself is
Having the
Experience of treating yourself as worthy and
Deserving of all the wonderful things life has to offer.

HOW CAN I BE MORE OF ME?

How you can be more of yourself is by

Opening to

What

Comes natural for you, not comparing yourself to others,

Allowing yourself to enjoy your

Natural talents and gifts, following your

Intuition and

Believing that you are here to

Experience joy in who God created you to be. The

More you

Offer yourself the

Right to experience your true self and

Express your natural talents, the more you create

Opportunities

For the

Magnificence of the real you to be

Experienced and expressed.

WHO IS MY AUTHENTIC SELF?

Who you are when you're
Having the experience of
Offering yourself from your
Innate nature, when you're
Sharing from your heart and
Moving in ways that
You
Are expressing and
Using your natural
Talents and abilities. You are authentic when you're
Honoring your natural self
Expression and
Not needing approval
To be who you are.
It's when you're
Creating from your uniqueness and
Shining the radiant light you are. Your authentic self
Expresses the
Love you are by
Following your hearts desires and your unique pattern.

HOW CAN I LIVE MORE AS MY AUTHENTIC SELF?

How can I live more as my authentic self?
One day at a time is
What you
Can do,
And continue to stay in the
Now moment.
In every situation see with the eyes of
Love and
Invite spirit to assist you as you
Venture into life.
Embrace each
Moment as a new beginning,
Open to the freshness of today and
Remember that today is all there really is.
Expressing your uniqueness, compassion
And love is living as your authentic
Self.
Much of the world is hurting.
You can be the change you want to see
As you stay true to your heart.
Unless you choose different
Today, you are already authentic,
Here, now.
Embrace your uniqueness and
Never give up on yourself.
Today, tomorrow and the future
Is filled with infinite possibilities.
Could you remain open to
See what life has in store for you?
Eventually you will be in alignment with the
Love you are, your authentic self and this love lasts
Forever.

HOW CAN I BE MORE SELF EMPOWERED?

Honor yourself and every

Opportunity you have.

Whenever you feel you

Can't do something,

Acknowledge the

Newness of the moment and

Invite divine wisdom to

Be with you and your

Experiences.

Make new choices in the present moment by

Opening your mind,

Reaching into your heart and seeing

Every experience as fresh and new.

Self empowerment comes from

Exploring

Life and

Following your inner wisdom. Soon you will

Experience

More of your own

Power.

Other people

Won't and can't create your self

Empowerment, you are the one who

Re-creates or creates your

Experiences. Being self empowered is allowing your

Divine nature to lead the way.

HOW CAN I BE AN INDEPENDENT ADULT?

Here is an
Opportunity
Where you
Can be an independent
Adult by honoring your
Needs and honoring yourself.
It's possible to
Become the
Experience of
An independent adult by
Naturally following your
Intuition, information that comes
Naturally from your
Divine center.
Every
Person
Experiences
Needs, it's up to you to
Decide how you will get them met.
Eventually your
Needs will be
Taken care of in
A way that you
Decide to
Use your life energy to
Love yourself enough to want
To take care of yourself.

WHAT DOES SELF RESPECT MEAN?

When you have self respect you are
Honoring yourself,
All of your experiences and speaking your
Truth. When you are
Doing things that
Offer you the opportunity to
Express yourself authentically and you're
Standing strong in who you are. When you're
Staying present in your
Experiences and allowing
Love to
Flow through you. When you're
Reversing negative
Expressions to positive ones and you're
Supporting and honoring yourself instead of
People pleasing. When you're
Enjoying all parts of your
Creative self and you're
Trusting in your
Magnificence. The
Experience of self respect is honoring
All of who you are right
Now.

HOW CAN I APPRECIATE MYSELF MORE?

Honor your divinity and

Offer yourself love

Whenever and wherever possible.

Create your life from the

Awareness that you have the option to be

Nice to yourself now, in this moment.

In this

Awareness

Place your love on any

Parts inside of yourself that are hurting.

Reach into your heart and

Embrace yourself fully.

Create a habit of

Inviting love into

All parts of your being

Today and

Everyday and soon all your experiences will involve

More love and appreciation for

Yourself and others.

Stay open and receptive to having

Experiences of

Love and

Forgive yourself and anyone who has

"Made" you upset.

Offer yourself appreciation by letting go of

Resistance and loving and

Embracing yourself and others unconditionally.

WHAT IS THE MEANING OF CONTROL?

What control
Has to do with is
A way
That you do things
In which helps you
See and feel
That you
Have power in your
Experience,
Meaning, you want to
Experience things in
A way that you
Notice comfort and familiarity,
In a way that you
Need to know what's
Going to happen so you
Offer a way to
Fulfill your need by
Controlling; which
Oppresses what can happen
Naturally.
The other meaning might be
Resistance to change. See this as an
Opportunity to learn to trust in the
Love of the divine.

HOW CAN I RELEASE THE NEED TO CONTROL?

Here is an
Opportunity to notice
What you're afraid of. Wanting to
Control is usually
A reaction to a fear of
Not knowing what
Is going to happen.
Right now allow yourself to
Experience what it would be
Like to
Experience a feeling of love
And safety. Take a deep breath, close your eyes, relax and
Surrender, breathe in love and breathe out love;
Express to yourself
That everything is going to be okay, that you are safe.
Having this new
Experience will
Naturally move you into the
Experience of
Experiencing safety in the love of the
Divine.
Today is a new
Opportunity where you
Can
Offer yourself a more
Natural way of allowing yourself
To
Release the fear and the illusion of control and
Open to the
Love and safety of the divine.

WHAT DOES IT MEAN TO TAKE RISKS?

When you are

Having

An experience

That you

Don't feel safe, you call it a risk, however, it's an

Opportunity to

Experience

Something new and create a sense of self-empowerment.

If you can see

That taking risks are

Meant to help you, then

Every risk you take is

An opportunity for you to

Notice your strengths.

Taking any challenge

Opens new doors of opportunities

That can expand your

Awareness and build your confidence and self esteem.

Keep in mind that new

Experiences are just that, new.

Risks are new experiences

In which you aren't

Sure what the outcome will be.

Kool and exciting experiences can happen by

Stepping into the unknown and taking risks.

IS THERE ANYTHING I NEED TO KNOW?

In this moment
Stay open, you're starting
To trust more.
Have each experience be
Right for you. It's not the
Experience but how you
Are experiencing it.
Notice when
You
Think that you
Have to do something
In a certain time and a certain way and
Notice how it
Gives you an anxious feeling.
If you can let go of the
Need to know and you allow your
Experiences to flow
Easily and naturally, the
Divine can
Then
Offer you what you need.
Keep in mind that when you let go of the
Need to know, it allows divine intelligence to
Offer you a
Way that is more in alignment with your divine purpose.

EXPECT THE BEST, STAY IN THE MOMENT

Expecting the best means allowing your
Xperiences to be filled with joy. It's
Placing your attention on
Expecting everything to be
Created in your favor.
Today is an opportunity
To
Have the awareness that
Everything is always working out for you. When you
Believe that your life
Experience is supposed to be good, you'll start to
See the good in all of your experiences.
Trusting in the Universe allows you to
Stay peaceful in
The moment,
Allowing
Your life to flow more easily and naturally.
It's when you stay in the
Now moment that you are more able
To
Have access to the fullness of your true
Essence.
Move into your experiences today with an
Open heart and intend to live in joy in each
Moment.
Expansion is taking place
Now, everything is always working out for you,
Trust the universe, let go and allow yourself to live in joy.

IS THERE ANYTHING THAT NEEDS MY ATTENTION?

In this time you are
Starting
To
Have
Experiences that are creating
Resistance,
Experiences where you
Are
Noticing
Your patterns and seeing
The thoughts, feelings and perceptions that you've held
Inside and haven't wanted to acknowledge and
Nothing is
Giving you comfort.
This is a time that you
Have to go through in order to
Awaken
To your true
Nature. The
Experiences that you are having are
Experiences that are helping you to understand your
Divine nature; they are opportunities that are
Showing you where in the past you've
Made
Yourself
A "bad" person because of
The
Thoughts you were thinking and/or the actions you were taking.
Experiencing this is
Necessary in order for you
To heal,
It's coming up for you to notice it so you can
Offer yourself a
New reality.

WHY AM I RESISTANT?

What's

Happening is

You

Aren't being truthful about

Moving

In a new direction, there's

Resistance inside, you might consider that you want your

Experiences to

Stay the same, there's some

Internal conflict that's

Stopping you. If you take time now

To talk to that part that's resisting without judgment

And see what it

Needs and why it's resisting, and you offer it compassion,

This will help you let go of resistance.

HOW CAN I HEAL THIS RIGHT NOW?

Here is an
Opportunity
Where you
Can
Assist yourself in
Noticing when you tighten
Inside and
Have the
Experience itself let you become
Aware of what you're
Learning
Through this experience, meaning
Having this experience
Is
Showing you a
Response that
Isn't in alignment with what you truly want to
Give your energy to and experience in your life and it
Has to speak
To you through this way.
Notice this as your body
Offering you a way to see
What is really going on.

WHAT IS THE RESISTANCE ABOUT?

Why you are

Having resistance is that you have

A competing part of you

That

Is

Scared because it feels

That if you share your creativity you

Have to have it perfect and it doesn't feel that it's perfect

Enough and it's creating the

Resistance. It's

Expressing resistance as a way to

Say to you that

It feels pressured by you that it has to be

Successful and receive recognition from others in order

To share.

Allowing yourself to

Notice this is giving you the opportunity to choose to

Create because your spirit wants to.

Express to the part of you that feels pressured that you

Are now allowing it to create

Because it feels good and

Offer yourself/it love and acceptance. Allow the

Universe to bring forth what is necessary as you continue

To create for the joy of being a channel for the divine.

WHAT IS PROCRASTINATION?

What

Happens when you

Are procrastinating is

That you don't feel that you deserve to have what

It is that is in front of you, you feel someone else

"Should" do it for you or you fear the experience.

Procrastination is a way that you try to

Resist the experience.

Out of procrastinating you are

Creating

Resistance which can be

A way of self

Sabotage that might be coming from a belief

That you aren't capable or worthy.

It is a perspective and belief that

Needs changing to be more in

Alignment with your

True self

In which you become

One with your natural self who is

Naturally worthy, loving and free flowing.

HOW HAVE I BEEN LIMITING MYSELF?

How you've limited yourself in the past was by

Obtaining

What you already know.

Having

A new

Vision is

Expressing to you that you are

In a time of

Becoming something new. You are ready to

Express what you have inside and share your authentic

Expression.

Notice the ways in which you

Let situations or beliefs formed

In the past

Make you feel

Intimidated, insecure or not good enough.

Today

Is an opportunity to create

New ways to see, experience and share your natural

Gifts and talents.

Move into

Your experiences today

Seeing with the eyes of Love. Let yourself

Experience the

Love of the Divine

Flowing through you into all you are and all that you do.

HOW CAN I RELEASE LIMITATIONS?

Here is an
Opportunity
Where you
Can see
All that you think you
Need
In order to "feel safe."
Releasing limitations is an
Experience of
Letting go, an
Experience that
Allows
Surrender, an
Experience that
Lets
In
More trust.
In
Trusting you
Are allowing
The universe to bring you what's
Intended for you,
Opportunities that are a
Necessary part of your
Spiritual evolution.

HOW DO I FIND TRUE FREEDOM?

How do I find true freedom?

Open your heart and live in love.

Whatever happens around you

Doesn't determine who you are.

Other people are living the way they choose.

Ignite your passion and allow it to

Flow through you

Into the world while

Noticing your

Divinity.

True freedom comes when you

Reach within

Underneath the façade to please

Everyone and you allow your true self to shine.

Freedom begins when you

Release the need for approval and you

Embrace yourself, everyone and

Everything as the

Divine

Offering its

Magnificence.

WHAT DOES IT MEAN TO LIVE IN FREEDOM?

What does it mean to live in freedom?

Here and now is all there is.

Answer the call of love

That resides within you and

Dance your

Own dance, everyone else is dancing theirs.

Everyone has their own unique rhythm and

Song in their heart.

Ignite the love inside your heart and allow it

To express and

Move through you.

Experiencing freedom is

Allowing your spirit, your

Natural self and your heart

To guide you. You have

Options every moment of everyday to

Live

In freedom.

Valuing and

Expressing your uniqueness

Is the most freeing and

Natural way of living. Living in

Freedom is

Remembering the truth about you and your unique

Expression. You are loved and you are

Enough, you don't have to prove this, you are perfectly

Designed. You are a unique expression

Of God, you are

Made from God, as God, celebrate this Loving Oneness.

HOW CAN I LIVE FREELY?

How you can live freely is by

Opening to

What's here, right now, in this moment, loving and

Caring

About yourself and others, seeing the beauty of

Nature

In you, through you and all around you,

Letting yourself love and be loved, being

In the flow and

Valuing your life

Experience. Living

Freely comes from

Realizing that your life

Experience is a gift and that

Everyday you are alive you have the opportunity to

Live in Gratitude and Love for

Yourself, others and your life experience.

HOW CAN I FIND PEACE WITHIN?

How can I find peace within?

Overcome fear of other people.

Walk hand and hand with god, have

Courage to be the real you

And accept that you are already perfect.

Notice when you

Identify with negative thoughts and state the truth instead.

Forgive yourself and others and

Invite peace and love to flow into the

Now moment. Pay attention to

Divine

Presence and

Embrace each opportunity

As something new to learn about yourself and others.

Celebrate your lessons and blessings.

Embrace divine love and

Watch yourself become more peaceful.

It's through love and acceptance

That you will learn to

Have peace no matter what

Is happening. Living in peace is your divine

Nature.

<u>HOW CAN I KEEP MY HEART OPEN?</u>

Honor every person, place and experience and

Offer love to

Whatever is happening now.

Create from the

Awareness that love is here

Now and everything else

Is an illusion, a story.

Knowing this and bringing this knowing into your

Experiences will help you

Experience love and keep your heart open.

Place your attention on

Making love for

Yourself and others a priority and this will keep your

Heart open. When you are

Experiencing love, your heart

Automatically opens and

Resistance falls away.

This will

Offer love and

Peace in you, through you and into all of your

Experiences easily and

Naturally.

WHAT IS THE MEANING OF GUILT?

When you are
Having
A feeling of guilt, it is
Telling you that you are
In a
State of blaming yourself for something
That
Happened in the past, an
Experience where you
Made yourself wrong. The
Experience of guilt can be unexpressed resentment
And is keeping you out of the present moment.
Notice that
In this moment
No one is
"Giving" you guilt. Guilt can also be a form
Of self sabotage and a block to the
Flow of love. You can't change the past, however,
Grace and forgiveness invites you to
Use your energy
In a way that brings peace and
Love into your life
Today.

WHAT IS THE GUILT ABOUT TODAY?

Where you
Have guilt is
Allowing yourself
To
Include your
Self in your life.
The guilt comes from
Having the misunderstanding that
Embracing and
Giving to yourself
Uses the energy that you "should" give to others.
In this misunderstanding/perception you've used your
Life energy
To focus on others
And now you're
Becoming aware that you want to
Offer your energy to be
Used in ways
That you are honoring yourself.
Today is an
Opportunity for you to forgive yourself,
Decide to release the guilt and any resentment,
And choose to honor yourself by giving
Yourself permission to allow yourself to be a priority.

THE POWER OF SUGGESTION

Take a moment to see where you

Have your attention. Most of your

Experiences are happening because of where you're

Placing your attention.

Offer yourself

What you need to have positive

Experiences

Right now.

Out of your words and thoughts your life will

Flow.

Say good-bye to any negativity and

Use the present moment to

Give yourself positive suggestions that will

Give your mind and body a way to create positive

Experiences.

Stay in tune with love and let go of fear,

Take your attention off

Illness and focus

On health, strength and wholeness

Now and fill every cell and fiber of your being with LOVE.

I FEEL FAT, WHY IS FAT AN ISSUE?

If you are

Feeling fat it's an

Experience from the past.

Explore the

Life you had when

Fat became

An issue and what you

Told yourself and concluded it meant about you.

What

Happens when

You feel fat is you are

In a

State of

Fear.

Allow

The fear to be

An awareness and

Notice

It as a

Scared part, the

Shadow that wants

Understanding, love and to

Express itself.

WHAT WAS I LEARNING FROM THE ANOREXIA?

Why you
Had
Anorexia was that you created a way for you
To feel safe and protected in a
World that seemed so overwhelming
And confusing, however it was actually
Self sabotage. Even though
It provided for you a way of
Life in which you thought that
Everything would be okay, it was
Actually a way that you were
Resisting having anything good in life and what you
Needed for true fulfillment.
In a sense you
Needed to
Go through this contrast in order
Find your strength,
Real love and true fulfillment.
Once you
Made the decision that it wasn't serving you anymore and
That you wanted to start to
Honor yourself so you could
Experience a more fulfilling life, you
Allowed yourself to do what was
Necessary in
Order to heal. Through your process of healing you've come to
Realize that the true
Experience of love and safety comes from within, from
Xperiencing a connection with the divine and having experiences
In which you are believing you are worthy and you're honoring, loving
And valuing yourself and all of your life experiences.

WHY DO I SECOND GUESS MYSELF

Whenever you
Have interactions with people
You feel you
Don't
Offer them what they want and
It makes you not want to
Share anymore.
Expectations of yourself or what you think you "should" say
Creates a way to
Offer yourself disapproval.
Notice when you think that you
Don't
Give the "right" words and
Understand that you might have
Expectations of yourself to
Say the right thing or not
Say anything at all. This
Makes
You want to hide and
Stay away from people. See if you can find the
Experience that created this belief,
Let yourself experience that experience and then
Find a new perception that brings you love and acceptance.

WHAT IS PEOPLE PLEASING?

When you are people pleasing you are
Having
A
Time
In which you might feel frightened to
Speak your truth.
People pleasing is an
Experience that
Offers other
People power over your
Life
Experience.
People pleasing is a way in which you
Let others
Experience what they want
And you
Stagnate in your own fulfillment.
It's okay for you to honor yourself sweetie; let your
Natural self be expressed;
Give yourself permission to be true to yourself.

WHAT'S A NEW PERCEPTION I CAN HAVE?

What new perception you can

Have is

A perception

That you are

Safe and that you are strong

And capable of

Naturally

Expressing the uniqueness of

Who you are. This

Perception allows you to

Experience,

Reveal and

Create from your natural abilities.

Expectations to do things

Perfect

Tend to get

In the way. Today is an

Opportunity for you to embrace your

Natural strengths and to

Include them in

Creating the life you desire. Using your natural

Abilities allows you to experience what is

Necessary for you to

Honor

And

Value your authentic

Expression.

HOW CAN I RELEASE THE NEED FOR APPROVAL?

Here you have the
Option to believe
What others say so you
Can have
Approval or you can approve of your
Natural expression.
It's up to you
Right now to
Experience
Love for yourself from yourself and the divine or
Expect it from
Another.
See where you need people to
Express
That they approve of you.
Have
Every experience help you to
Notice what you
Expect from others in order to
Experience being loved and approved of.
Decide today and everyday that you are
Filled with divine love.
Open yourself to this love,
Reach within and
Allow love to expand throughout your entire being.
Place your attention
Past
Recognition from
Others and
Value yourself by walking in the world with
A knowing that you are already
Loved and approved of.

HOW CAN I BE MORE COMPASSIONATE WITH ME?

How you can be more compassionate is by
Offering yourself love
Where you judged yourself in the past.
Can you
Allow yourself to be like
Nature and love yourself just as you are, as god created you?
It's when you judge yourself you are
Believing that your
Expression is wrong.
Much
Of your pain
Right now comes from
Expressing judgment.
Could you
Offer yourself
More compassion by
Putting less pressure on yourself
And know that life is a work in progress.
Seek to do your best as you
Stay
In tune with love.
Offering yourself the idea that you
Need
Approval and perfection
Tends to create the
Experience
Where you judge yourself as not being good enough.
Its
The judgment that
Has to be
Moved out of the way and be replaced with the
Experience of compassion and love.

<u>*YOU ARE LOVED AND APPRECIATED*</u>

YOU ARE LOVED and APPRECIATED.
Opening to the Love of the Divine is the
Ultimate
And
Richest
Experience of
Love. When you
Open to this love and allow it to flow through you,
Vibrationally you will be uplifting humanity by
Experiencing and expressing the LOVE of the
Divine.
Assume right
Now that
Divine light
And love is flowing through you.
Place your attention on any
Places inside that might feel unloved
Right now and allow yourself to
Experience this flow of Love moving through you.
Cherish and embrace
Infinite love that is
Always flowing and
Thank the Universe for this opportunity to
Experience Life and the Love of the
Divine.

WHAT DOES IT MEAN TO BE SAFE?

What does it mean to be safe?

How do I create safety

And how do I know

That I am safe?

Does my heart

Open up to

Everyone and everything? Is

Success safety or is it an

Illusion of safety?

Trust in yourself and

Make love be your safety.

Eventually you'll become more

Aware that

Nothing outside yourself can bring you safety.

Trust in the spirit of love that's already inside you.

Open yourself to this love

Because true safety resides within you.

Everything else is an illusion of

Safety. Bring your

Awareness to the divine being you are and

Feel the love from the core of your being and fill

Every cell in body with this love; this is true safety.

HOW CAN I CREATE SAFETY IN A POSITIVE WAY?

Having safety is
Offering yourself love
Where you've judged yourself in the past.
Creating safety is
A way that comes
Natural when you are
In tune with your
Creator.
Realize that
Every time you
Are in fear or judgment it
Takes you out of the
Experience of love and
Safety.
A
Feeling of safety comes from the
Experience within you,
The experience that
You are safe with yourself.
It's
Necessary to feel safe with yourself, then you'll be more
Able to feel safe with other
People.
Offering love to yourself creates
Safety.
If you don't feel safe
Then
It's probably because you're not
Valuing yourself.
Expressing love and appreciation to yourself
Without judgment creates
A way for
You to feel loved and safe.

WHAT IS THE BELIEF ABOUT TRUST?

What's

Happening is you

Are believing that

Trust

Is when

Situations

Turn out exactly

How you plan. These

Expectations cause you to

Believe that all

Experiences should be

Lived

In accordance to your

Expectations and this creates

Fear. Becoming

Aware of this

Belief

Offers you

Understanding as to why in

The past it was difficult for you

To trust. Be aware that trust doesn't always mean comfort.

Right now you have the opportunity to create a new

Understanding of trust that

Says

That all is Divine.

HOW CAN I MAKE TRUST A PRIORITY?

Here is an

Opportunity

Where you

Can

Allow yourself what's

Necessary

In order to

Move into the

Awareness of when you

Keep going back to familiar ways to

Experience safety.

Trust will come when you are ready to

Release resistance and you truly

Understand and experience love. Love brings feelings of

Safety; when you feel safe you're more able to

Trust. When you are trusting you are

Allowing the

Present situation to

Reveal to you what

Is being

Offered in the moment.

Right now is an opportunity to

Intend to

Trust by allowing

Yourself to experience Loving Oneness with all of life.

ACTIONS SPEAK LOUDER THEN WORDS

Actions speak louder then words
Could be
That you are noticing ways
In which you see
Other people behaving.
Notice this
Situation as a mirror
Showing you the ways that you are functioning.
People are showing you the
Experiences that
Are similar to the
Kind of ways that you are living your
Life. Seeing it in
Others is offering you insight into
Understanding the ways that you say things but they
Don't match your
Experiences.
Right now
This situation is
Having you look at how the things you
Express and what you do are different.
Notice this as an opportunity to see
What needs to be healed in you in
Order for you to follow through with what you
Really want. Notice your actions,
Do they match your words?
Synchronize them and watch what happens.

IS THERE ANYTHING BLOCKING ME NOW?

If this situation
Scares you
Then
Have a moment to
Experience the
Resistance or fear; allow yourself to
Experience what you
Are feeling
Now, in this present moment.
Your feelings are
Telling you that you might be
Having an
Internal conflict.
Notice what is
Going on inside
Before you
Let yourself
Offer yourself that notion that you
Can't do something.
Keep
In mind that by
Noticing what you're feeling it
Gives you an opportunity to create a new
Meaning. A feeling really wants to be felt and
Experienced. This experience is helping you
Notice what's happening inside. It's an
Opportunity for you to notice
Where you might be stuck in a misunderstanding.

HOW CAN I MOVE THROUGH THE FEAR?

Here you can see where you
Offer yourself fear and
What
Causes the fear.
Ask yourself if it's
Necessarily real
In the
Moment or if it's a negative assumption/anticipation.
Out of being
Vulnerable you'll be able to
Experience that
The fear comes from the past, something unknown or
Having a thought that you're not safe.
Right now
Offer yourself
Understanding by
Giving yourself the opportunity to see
How you bring the past or
The anticipation of a future outcome into the now.
Help yourself by becoming present, close your
Eyes, focus on your heart and say "I am safe."
From this moment on replace the
Expression of fear with becoming
Aware of the present moment, focusing on your heart and
Reminding yourself that all is well.

WHAT FEAR CAN I RELEASE RIGHT NOW?

What fear you can release
Has to do with
A
Time when you
Followed your heart and your
Experience felt like
A
Rejection.
Can you see the ways in which you
Are rejecting yourself now?
Notice how
Inside you are
Rejecting yourself because of something you used to believe.
Explore the ways in which you
Let a misunderstanding from your past filter your
Experiences today.
Awareness is the first
Step in changing your
Experiences today. How you can
Release the fear of rejection
Is to
Give love,
Honor and acceptance
To yourself and re-connect to the
Nature
Of your being
Who is already accepted and Loved.

WHY AM I AFRAID TO GET ANGRY, WHY?

When you
Have anger
You get frightened because you think that you
Are bad if you are angry and that being angry
Might make someone mad at you.
If you can
Allow yourself to
Feel the anger instead of
Resisting it, you might find it to be
A relief, that
Is, in the past you
Didn't
Trust it so you did the
Opposite, you held it in which
Gave you the
Experience of anxiety and made you
Tired. If you
Are afraid
Notice the fear and also notice any judgments that are
"Giving" you the feeling of anger.
Realize that the anger that
You are having is a message from
Within. It's telling you that you
Have a certain belief that
You are attached to from the past.

WHAT WAS MY DREAM TELLING ME?

What
Happened in your dream was
Anger,
That
What you wanted wasn't
Anything close to what you got and you concluded that it
Said that you didn't
Matter, that no one thinks of
You or gives you what you want.
Decide to see what was being
Revealed to you, that your
Experience in your dream was
A way for you to see the
Meaning you put on your experiences
Today, that the
Experience in your dream was
Letting you know how you view
Life
In the
Now, that you feel you don't matter.
Give yourself the opportunity to create a new
Meaning by treating yourself like you matter and watch how your
Experiences change.

HOW CAN I SHOW MYSELF THAT I MATTER?

Here is an

Opportunity

Where you

Can show yourself you matter by

Allowing yourself to have

Needs and

In that

See what it's like to

Have experiences where you are honoring your needs and

Offer yourself love from

Within. Feeling like you

Matter comes from the way that

You treat your

Self. Place your hand on your heart, tune into your

Essence and say out loud "I matter!"

Let yourself

Feel what it's like

To say this.

Have this new expression become

A way for you to hear truth. State it often

Throughout the day from this space of love.

In this you will be

Moving into

Alignment with your

True self, because the

Truth is you do matter, your life and

Expression is the

Radiance of the divine.

HOW CAN I HEAL THE FEELING OF ABANDONMENT?

How you can heal this is by becoming aware of the
O*ccurrence in*
W*hich you had that*
C*reated*
A feeling of abandonment.
N*otice the ways*
I*n which you*
H*ave the*
E*xperience of*
A*bandonment now. Become aware of how you've*
L*et*
The feeling that was created in the past
H*ave an impact on the way you are*
E*xperiencing your life today.*
F*or instance; the feeling that you're*
E*xperiencing now came from a prior*
E*xperience and perception; you might want to consider*
L*ooking at the ways*
I*n which you may feel abandoned by god as well as*
N*oticing how you might be abandoning yourself. By*
G*iving the*
O*ffering of*
F*orgiveness and love to yourself, god*
And those whom you
B*elieve*
Abandoned you, you'll be able to re-connect with your
N*atural love which is*
D*ivine love and divine love*
O*ffers you full acceptance. Connecting to the divine*
N*aturally*
M*oves you into the*
E*xperience of being*
N*urtured;*
The experience of being cared for and loved.

WHY AM I AFRAID TO CHANGE?

What

Happens when

You come upon change you get

Afraid because the word change

Makes you believe that something bad

Is going to happen

And that creates

Fear and

Resistance. If you truly believe

All

Is

Divine

Then the

Opportunity for

Change can be a

Happy experience

And you will be able to

Notice and embrace the

Gift of the

Experience of change.

WHAT CHANGES ARE HAPPENING THAT ARE NECESSARY?

What's
Happening is you're becoming very
Aware
That
Change is necessary but you don't know
How
And the
Need to know how is
Giving you anxiety and creating resistance.
Express faith in the divine and you'll be
Shown the how when you
Are
Ready to
Experience what's necessary.
Have this experience right now be
A way for you to be
Present. Experiencing
Presence allows truth to be
Expressed. The
Now moment is a new moment which
Includes the
Natural flow of the process,
Giving you the opportunity
To trust that everything
Happens in divine order and
Allows you
To feel more accepting of change
And new beginnings.
Right now is all there is,
Explore this
Now moment and allow new
Experiences to
Come into your life.
Expect them, and
Stay open to the idea that your
Spirit is free flowing and
Allow yourself to feel the
Richness of who
You truly are.

WHAT ARE THE PATTERNS FROM PREVIOUS JOBS?

What you
Had
As patterns were
Trust issues
And
Relating to others. The
Experiences
That you
Had were
Experiences where you allowed
People to hurt you.
Arranging those situations reflected
The ways in which you were hurting yourself.
Today, your
Experiences are being
Renewed. You're now willing to love,
Nurture and care for yourself and you're attracting new
Situations that
Feel good and that are now
Right for you. You're now creating new
Opportunities that are
Moving from the
Place you were and you're allowing yourself to have
Richer
Experiences of loving and
Valuing yourself and others.
Inviting new
Opportunities, new
Understandings and new ways of
Seeing helps you to notice the ways that you
Justified your past experiences. You are now ready to
Offer yourself the
Belief that you are
Sacred and that you deserve to be treated with LOVE.

WHAT ARE SOME SOLUTIONS FOR ME NOW?

What's happening

Has to do with

A

Time in the past when you

Agreed/misunderstood that other people were

Right, that your

Expression

Shouldn't be

Offered because it

Made people mad and now you

Expect that the

Same thing will happen if you express.

Out of this experience/misunderstanding you've

Let yourself become

Useless, meaning, you've hid your true expression.

Today

Is a new day,

Offer yourself what you

Need to forgive those who

Said that and

Forgive yourself for accepting that as truth. This is an

Opportunity to believe something new

Right now,

Meaning, let go of

Expectations and beliefs from the past, be here

Now and

Offer yourself love, acceptance and the opportunity to

Win your true self back and the freedom to express yourself.

WHAT IS THE TRUTH ABOUT EXPRESSING?

When you
Have
An opportunity
To express
Its
Saying
That you're
Honoring yourself, God and your life
Experience;
The ways in which you naturally express
Reveal the
Understanding of your
True nature. When you
Honor who God created you to be, you're
Allowing the truth of your
Being to be revealed. Today is an
Opportunity to
Use your natural talents and gifts
To express your true nature. This
Experience of wanting to
Xpress is
Present because you are
Ready to
Experience, express and
Share your true
Self.
It's your divine purpose to share your
Natural talents and
Gifts with the world.

WHAT CAN I DO TO EXPRESS TODAY?

What's

Happening right now is

A way

That your

Creativity

And intuition is

Naturally expressing.

It's a

Decision that you've made to

Open yourself to receive guidance and allow it to flow

To and through you

Offering ways for you to

Experience healing and share it with others. Every

Xperience in life

Presents a way for you to

Reveal your

Expression.

Seeing the many ways that

Spirit wants

To shine through you

Opens

Doors that

Allows

Your true expression to flow.

I'M UNCOMFORTABLE, HOW CAN I CONNECT TO LOVE?

In this
Moment you are
Understanding how you
Need
Comfort and this
Opportunity is offering you
Much discomfort and
Fear. Notice how you
Offer
Resistance when it's
Time to change
And move in a new direction.
Be willing to
Let yourself
Experience what you're feeling.
Have this
Opportunity be a
Way in which you learn what you
Call
Allowing.
Not every experience
Is going to be easy, however, you
Can always
Open to the love inside.
Needing every experience to be easy blocks what you
Need to learn, grow and heal. All of your
Experiences contain a
Certain lesson and blessing.
Today, allow each experience
To be a way that you
Offer
Love to yourself with
Out conditions. You are still
Valuable and lovable
Even if you feel uncomfortable.

WHY DO I FEEL SO ANXIOUS RIGHT NOW?

What's
Happening is
You're focusing on
Doing instead of being.
Offer yourself permission to just be
Instead of always having to do.
Flow with the
Experience of what's happening now.
Everything's going to be okay sweetie.
Love,
Surrender and trust,
Open your heart
And allow
Now to be perfect as it is, anything
Xtra
Is creating anxiety and
Obstructing your peace.
Use your energy to
Stay present
Right now.
In this you are
Going with the flow,
Honoring yourself and
This time, allowing your life to
Naturally unfold in divine order with the
Opportunity to flow easily and graciously
With the process of life.

WHAT'S THE DEEPER MEANING HERE?

What you

Have

As a deeper meaning is that you are

Taking things too

Seriously and you're creating stories

That

Have you fearing your

Experiences.

Decide today that you will let yourself

Experience your life

Experiences by

Placing your attention on viewing your

Experiences.

Realizing that

Much of your life

Experience is happening through the ways you

Are thinking gives you the opportunity to

Notice how you can

Include whatever story you want.

Noticing that you are the creator allows you to

Give whatever meaning you want to your experiences.

How you relate to yourself while going through your

Experiences is the key.

Remember that every thought has a reaction in your

Experience.

WHY DO I FEEL SO BAD RIGHT NOW?

Why you feel bad

Has to do with

Your

Decision to

Offer yourself wrong

Insight.

Find the

Experience that created the

Expression that

Let you

See that you were an

Object of imperfection.

Believing this gave you

A way that you

Decided to hurt yourself. Allow your true self to be

Revealed by going

Inside yourself and

Giving

Honor

To your divine

Nature, the beauty and perfection that you are and

Offer love and acceptance to

Where you were hurting.

WHY DID I CREATE A FALSE SELF?

When you were young and you

Had feelings of not being loved

You

Decided that

If you

Did and said what you

Interpreted was "right" then you would be

Cared for and loved. By "trying" to be

Right you created a false self based on the

Expectations of others. By putting

All of your energy into

Trying to be loved you neglected your natural

Expression, formed layers of misunderstandings

And created a

False self. Take

A moment right now to forgive yourself for

Letting yourself believe that if you are your true

Self then you won't be loved. Your

Essence is made of love and

Since you're made of love the

Experience of love is who you are. Today

Let yourself experience and live

From and as your true self. YOU ARE LOVE!

WHAT SCARES ME ABOUT BEING ALIVE?

When you are

Having

A fear response

To being alive, you are

Saying that

Creating your life is too hard

And you're

Resisting your

Experiences.

Staying the same

Makes your

Energy stagnant, blocks the flow

And you

Begin to miss the amazing

Opportunities for you.

Understand that when you

Trust and

Believe that life can be a incredible

Experience, and you let your true self express,

It will allow what's

Necessary to come into your life and

Give you what you need to have a wonderful experience.

Align yourself with divine

Love and you'll naturally be

In tune with the

Value of your life

Experience.

WHY DO I RESIST EXPERIENCING LIFE?

What

Happened in the past was that

You had a under"lying" belief that you didn't

Deserve to live and out

Of that belief you

Included

Resisting anything that allowed you to

Experience the fullness of life.

See where you decided that you weren't good enough and that

It wasn't okay for you to enjoy life.

See

The meaning you created about yourself and life;

Examine what you believe about the ways you were "allowed" to

Xperience life.

Pause for a moment and allow yourself to

Experience and feel the

Resistance.

Is there a perception or misunderstanding about yourself and the

Experience of life that

Needs to be

Changed? Do you need to forgive yourself or another

In order for you to allow yourself to experience and enjoy life

Now? Give yourself a moment now to close your eyes,

Go into your heart and

Let yourself

Imagine a life where you are living

Fully, experiencing all you ever wanted to

Experience, smile and claim this for you now, you deserve it!

WHAT DO I NEED TO LEARN RIGHT NOW?

Where you are
Has to do with what you're thinking
About
Today.
Does your thinking
Offer you peace?
If you can let go of
Needing your
Experiences to be a certain way and you allow yourself to
Experience the process, not just focused on the
Destination,
Then you are learning. Life is about
Opening to the joy of the experience. In
Letting yourself enjoy the
Experience of who you are
And all you do, you will understand that the
Real purpose of life is to have experiences.
Noticing that life is a process and not an event
Releases you from pressuring yourself and
Instead you can be more relaxed and peaceful as you
Go with the flow.
Have the courage
To trust that all things work together for good. You are
Naturally guided and
Offered
What you need in the moment, so enjoy the process.

WHAT IS MY INTUITION TELLING ME?

What's
Happening is you
Are
Taking things
Into your own hands.
Surrender, you're
Making
Yourself
Insane and creating things that aren't
Necessary.
Today you are learning to
Understand your
Inner world.
Today you are
In a time
Of creating a
New life and it
Takes
Exceptional
Love and patience to
Let
In
New experiences.
Give yourself a chance to
Make new
Experiences a part of your life.

WHAT IS THE INHERENT MEANING?

What's
Happening is that you
Are
Trying too hard to feel that you're
Important.
See
This situation as being divinely ordered for you to
Have this
Experience to help you heal.
It's helping you to
Notice
How you
Expect a
Reason or validation from others in order for you to
Experience your importance.
Nature is
Telling you to let go of trying to
Make yourself important and allow yourself to
Experience who you
Are, a divine child of God.
Nature created you and who you are
Is already important; your
Natural self
Gives you your importance.

WHAT DO I NEED TO DO RIGHT NOW?

What you can do is

Have

A quiet

Time to

Do nothing. Take this

Opportunity to go

Inside yourself, to

Notice what your body is

Experiencing and

Expressing to you. If you are always

Doing you are

Taking away from the

Opportunity to

Decide how to

Offer yourself what feels

Right. By being quiet and going

Inside yourself you can

Get a more

Honest answer

To what's happening

Now and this will

Offer you

What you need.

WHAT IS MAKING ME UNCOMFORTABLE?

What's
Happening is you
Are
Trying to control
Instead of
Surrendering to what is. When you
Make your experiences
And yourself wrong,
Know that this
Is repressing what
Needs to be felt.
Give yourself permission to
Move through the
Experience, feel all your feelings and allow them to help you
Understand what might
Need love, forgiveness and/or
Correction.
Out of allowing your feelings to
Move through you, you will
Find an
Opportunity to see what you've been
Resisting, an opportunity
To be
Able to look at the
Beliefs that are creating your
Life
Experience now. Awareness is the first step.

HOW DO I SURRENDER MY WILL?

How you surrender your will is by

Opening to

What is here right now. Your

Desires manifest

Out of allowing them to happen

In perfect time and perfect order.

Since you are in the process of

Understanding what's

Real for you now

Rather than tainting your

Experiences based on perceptions from the past, you're

Naturally finding ways to

Design new

Experiences through what is being

Revealed to you through experiencing Loving Oneness.

Meaning, to surrender

Your

Will you are

In harmony with

Life and joining forces with the power of the universe,

Letting yourself relax and enjoy all of your experiences

HOW CAN I BE MORE AVAILABLE?

How you can be more available is by

Offering a

Way to

Cherish this moment.

All you

Need

Is right here, right now.

By being present you'll

Experience being

More available. It's an

Opportunity to

Release having to know, allowing yourself to

Experience what's here now

And loving yourself no matter what!

Valuing yourself and everything that's present

Allows you to be

In alignment with

Love which

Allows you to

Be more free flowing and

Lets you be more available in

Every experience.

WHAT ARE YOU GUIDING ME TO DO?

What I
Have
As guidance for you is
To sit quietly
And close your eyes.
Right now you can allow yourself to
Experience inner stillness by offering
Yourself the
Opportunity to
Use this moment to connect with
God.
Understand that
Its important to sit
Daily
In quietness. This
Naturally
Gives you
More then trying to make your
Experiences happen.
Today is an
Opportunity to be, to
Decide to slow down, let your thoughts flow and
Open to the divine.

WHAT ARE MY TRUE DESIRES?

When you
Have
A desire you are
Thinking
About and
Revealing the
Experience you want to have,
Meaning,
Your desires
That you are thinking about now are
Revealing a way to
Understand what you want to
Experience in your life.
Desires are
Expressions that your
Spirit
Intends to make
Real in your
Experiences through you
Senses.

IS THERE ANYTHING I CAN DO NOW?

In this moment
See that all
That is
Happening, all of your
Experiences
Right now are
Experiences intended for you.
Allow yourself to
Notice
Your
Thoughts and
How you
Interpret what's happening
Now.
Give your attention and
Intention to
Creating
Authentically and allow
Nature to bring you
Divine
Opportunities.
Notice what's being
Offered as a mirror of your internal
World

I'M FEELING TOTALLY REJECTED

If you are feeling rejected, you are putting

Meaning into the

Feelings and

Experience you had.

Experiencing a rejection

Lets you know that

Inside you

Need to

Give yourself more love.

The rejection you perceive

Outside can be a projection of your own rejection.

This is an opportunity to become

Aware of how you might be rejecting yourself.

Love yourself sweetie,

Let

Yourself

Really

Experience love for yourself right now.

Just because someone is

Expressing rejection towards you, you don't have to

Create a rejection

Towards yourself. Their

Expression is offering you a way to

Decide to love yourself even more, it's not about them.

HOW CAN I GET UNSTUCK TODAY?

Here is an
Opportunity for you to notice
What happens when you
Can't come up with
An answer.
Notice the ways
In which you
Give your attention and the energy behind it. It's
Essential
To see and
Understand the thoughts you
Nurture and the ways you feel. This
Situation is helping you
To see how you
Use your thoughts to
Create the
Kind of feelings you have.
This is an
Opportunity to
Decide to pause for
A moment, go into your heart and ask
Yourself "What would Love do?"

I FEEL VERY CONFUSED

If you are
Feeling confused you are
Experiencing what you need.
Every time you feel confused you are
Letting in new information that can be
Valuable. This
Experience is
Revealing to
You that when you're
Confused you are actually
Opening to
New information and insight that you
Find that you don't
Understand yet.
Surrender into to the
Experience with a knowing that all is
Divine.

HOW CAN I RELEASE FEAR OF EMBARRASSMENT?

Having Love for yourself
Offers you a
Way that you
Can be more
Accepting of yourself.
Notice
If what you think is
Real.
Everything in
Life is just an
Experience
At the time.
See if the
Experience of
Fear of embarrassment is an anticipation of an
Experience in which you
Are believing to be
Real, possibly from a past experience and/or perception. Today is an
Opportunity to
Find a new perception that can offer you the
Experience that
Makes you feel better.
Bring to mind something or someone you love
And
Right now place your attention on this feeling being
Real. In this experience you
Are creating a way for you to
See and
Sense how what you focus on creates the
Meaning you put on your
Experiences.
Notice that you can set yourself free by
Taking yourself into the loving.

WHERE AM I RESISTANT?

Why you are

Having the

Experience of

Resistance is that you are

Expecting that you

Are

Meant to be perfect, but according to who?

If you can let go of

Resisting the

Experience and

See this as an opportunity to

Invite a new way of life, then this

Situation is helping you

To change what you

Are believing to

Noticing

The greatness of your unique expression.

WHAT IS A NEW PERCEPTION I CAN HAVE?

What you can
Have
As a new perception is
That what
Is perfect is your
Soul. You
Are
Naturally perfect. Your
Experiences aren't
What makes you
Perfect; your soul's
Essence is what's perfect.
Right now focus on your essence, your divine
Creation, this is the
Experience of
Perfection.
Today be
In tune with the
Offering of your
Natural self as you
Invite life to
Create ways for you to
Allow yourself to
Notice and
Honor your
Authentic perfection.
Value your internal self as already perfect and notice how your
Experiences change.

HOW CAN I EXPAND MY AWARENESS?

Here is an

Opportunity

Where you

Can

Allow a wider truth that isn't

Necessarily present

In this moment.

Expanded awareness is giving you

Xtra room for more than what you see right now.

Place your

Attention on

Naturally expanding your awareness by opening to the

Divine and allowing it to

Move

You into

A bigger view, a

Way that you are

Aware of a bigger picture

Rather than what you're

Experiencing and seeing right

Now.

Expanded awareness is the ability to

See beyond what you are being

Shown through a limited perception or belief.

LIVING WITHOUT LIMITATIONS

Living without limitations
Is
Valuing that there is a choice
In every moment.
New choices allows the universe to
Give you new experiences.
With the ability to choose,
It's an opportunity
To
Have an
Opening to
Use your internal guidance,
To expand your awareness and
Let the
Internal you, the real you
Make choices.
It's an opportunity
To let go of
Attachment
To a story or of protecting an
Image or identity you held about yourself. Today is an
Opportunity to release old conditioning and allow your
Natural
Self to lead the way.

WHAT DO I NEED TO KNOW RIGHT NOW?

When you are
Having an
Awareness it gives you the opportunity
To see what you've been
Doing and the
Opportunity to change
If you choose. When you
Notice an
Experience that
Eludes you,
Do what is necessary
To see what's going on internally.
Opportunities to heal will
Keep showing up until you heal what
Needs to be healed.
Open yourself to
Whatever is present
Right now,
In this moment and
Give what is
Happening a way
To show you literally or symbolically what
Needs your attention, allow it to
Occur as it is and see
What you can learn and heal.

HOW CAN I BE MORE GENEROUS TODAY?

Here you can
Offer a
Way to
Care
About the
Needs
In the world
By
Expressing
More love, sharing your wealth and creativity and
Offering the
Real you to
Express as the
Giving spirit you are.
Expressing generosity is allowing
Nature to
Express through you with the
Realization of an abundant universe.
Offer yourself as a channel to
Uplift humanity by
Sharing from your heart and allowing gods energy
To move through you. Today is an
Opportunity to
Decide to
Allow yourself to live as the generous spirit
You are.

WHAT ARE THE REASONS TO BE GENEROUS?

When you are

Having

A

Time of generosity you

Are believing that you are

Rich and

Expressing

To the universe that you

Have. This

Enhances truth and brings forth more

Richness into your life.

Every generous gift

Allows you to

See that when you are

Offering, you are in tune with your

Natural

Self.

Today, when you

Offer,

Believe that

Every

Gift you give

Enhances your

Natural self and gives the

Experience of joy to you and the

Receiver. Giving is the

Opportunity to

Understand and express as your true

Self.

HOW CAN I BE MORE PATIENT WITH MY PROCESS?

Have you considered this time as an
Opportunity
Where you
Can
Allow
Nature to be
In charge? Know that you're
Being supported and all your
Experiences have a
Meaning and purpose. All of your experiences
Offer you something valuable.
Realizing that life is about
Experiencing, learning, growing and evolving will help you become more
Patient with your process
And allow what's necessary for your life experience
To happen
In divine order. Today is an opportunity to give yourself permission to
Experience the
Natural flow of
The process.
When you get
Impatient, remind yourself
That nothing
Happens before you're ready. Your outer world
Moves naturally when
Your inner world shifts. You're in the
Process of
Releasing
Outdated beliefs, perceptions and judgments and
Creating new ones that are more in alignment with the
Experience of your true self.
Surrender into the loving
Sweetie, everything is going to be okay, it's all divine.

EXPECTATIONS OR DISAPPOINTMENTS?

Expectations are
Xperiences where you
Place your attention on
Expecting things to be
Created in your favor and if
They don't happen the way you plan then you feel
A disappointment or rejection.
Today
Is an
Opportunity to
Notice this and to choose to
See it differently, it's an
Opportunity to
Remind yourself of your
Divine nature.
It's when you can
See that every person and experience is divine,
And you allow
People to be who they are without taking things personally or
Putting expectations on them or yourself, you'll be
Offered what
Is the
Natural flow of
The Universe.
Meaning; allowing lets your
Experiences flow more easily as you begin to
Notice the natural opening of your heart and
The free flowing and Loving
Spirit that you are.

WHAT DOES IT MEAN TO BE PERFECT?

When you are

Having

A moment

That you think that you

Didn't "Do it right" you can

Offer yourself a way to see it as an opportunity for learning.

Expecting yourself or your

Situations to be perfect

Is an illusion.

This

Means that in your

Experiences you

Are always learning.

Noticing this allows you

To accept everything as

Opportunities.

Bless

Each experience as

Perfectly designed for you.

Each time you make it or yourself wrong you're

Resisting the experience and/or lesson and obstructing the

Flow. All of your

Experiences are part of

Creation. All of creation is perfect, and

This means that you are too!

HOW CAN I VIEW MISTAKES NOW?

Here is an
Opportunity
Where you
Can
Allow yourself to
Notice that
If you allow mistakes and
View
It as a natural
Experience, you
Will begin to see that
Making mistakes
Is actually an opportunity to
See and experience a creative discovery. Sometimes
The mistake is
A way for you to notice something
Kool that you might not have
Experienced if you didn't make the "Mistake."
Seeing that mistakes are
Not bad, and are
Opportunities for awareness and/or correction
Will help you be open to experiencing all that life brings.

WHAT BELIEF AM I ATTACHED TO TODAY?

What's
Happening is that you
Are
Thinking and
Believing that your
Experience of
Life
Is an
Experience of
Failure and you
Are
Making your life
Into
A way of hiding and avoiding
The
Things that you can do because of the belief that you had been
Attached to based on a mis-perception from past experiences.
Can you now be willing to
Honor yourself by
Expressing love and acceptance instead of judgment? Will you
Decide to see that life is about learning and growing.
The perception of "failure" isn't true; you're being offered an
Opportunity for learning, to see a correction or adjustment.
Take a moment right now to imagine what it would be like to
Offer love and acceptance to yourself. What would you
Do, how would you feel, think and act. Take a deep breath
And now align yourself with this experience of loving
Yourself unconditionally.

WHAT BELIEF NEEDS TO GO?

What's

Happening right now is

A way

That's telling you that up until now you

Believed that your

Experience in

Life

Is supposed to be fearful. Somewhere you had an

Experience that told you that you were supposed to be

Fearful.

Now that you are aware of this, you can create a new

Experience. Imagine that

Everything in life is love and that

Divine love is

Supporting you and

Taking care

Of you. That

Gods arms are holding you and

Offering you all that you need to feel safe and loved.

WHAT ARE MY PATTERNS THAT NEED CHANGING?

*What's
Happening in your life is
Already changing naturally.
The patterns that
Are necessary to be changed are changing as you
Reveal more of your authentic
Expression,
Meaning,
You're now
Participating in life in
A more
Trusting way.
Today, your
Experiences are
Reflecting more of your
Natural
Self.
This is
How things change, when you
Are surrendering and
Trusting in
Nature and when you're living as and
Expressing from your
Essential self, your
Divine nature.
Creation
Has
A way of
Naturally
Giving you what
Is
Necessary at any
Given moment, keep surrendering and trusting.*

HOW CAN I OPEN TO FULFILLING MY DESIRES?

Here is an
Opportunity
Where you
Can be more
Aware of what you
Naturally desire.
In taking time to find
Out what you desire you will be
Presented with opportunities to
Experience a
Natural fulfillment of what you really want.
Today,
Offer yourself
Fulfillment by
Using the
Love
For what you desire to come
Into your life and
Let this
Love
Invite your desires
Naturally into your experiences.
Give this
Moment a way to give
Your attention to invite what you
Desire by saying; "What I desire is on its way and is coming into my
Experience in greater ways than I can imagine."
See
It in your mind and feel it with emotion as it being a
Real
Experience now, be open and receptive and
Say yes to receiving all that you desire.

<u>*ARE THERE ANY STEPS I CAN TAKE?*</u>

As you continue to
Realize what you want to
Experience
The
How will be shown.
Every
Realization allows you to
Experience
A
New reality.
You are being
Shown
The how and the steps to take through your
Experiences. The right
People, places, ideas and
Situations are showing up
In divine order.
Creation is
A
Natural process.
Trust
And surrender to the process,
Keep on creating,
Expressing and visioning your dreams and desires.

WHAT IS MY SOUL TRYING TO REVEAL?

What's
Happening is you
Are
Trying to be
In two places at once.
Start by
Making
Your life
Simple by
Offering yourself this moment and
Using the resources that are already inside you.
Life is
Teaching you that when you
Resist change
You
Interfere with what's
Needing to happen.
Give yourself
Time and see that
Opportunities will
Reveal themselves as you
Enter into a
Vision of your true
Expression
And you
Live in the moment.

WHAT IS MY SOUL SEEKING TO LEARN?

What's
Happening is you
Are in a
Time
In which you are starting to
See differently, you're noticing how
Much of
Your life is based on what you
Sense and you're now able to
Offer yourself and others
Understanding, compassion and
Love.
Seeing your
Experiences more clearly is helping you. Every
Experience offers you an opportunity to experience a
Kind of trust that allows you to see
In each situation that
Not all the information is
Given to you at the
Time. You are now having more
Opportunities to
Love and be loved without
Expectations because you
Are allowing yourself to be,
Radiate and experience your
Natural essence, which is LOVE.

WHAT DOES MY SOUL WANT TO EXPRESS?

What does my soul want to express?

Honor yourself and become

Aware of your infinite potential.

Today you are recognizing that you are perfectly

Designed to be you. Infinite

Opportunities are in front of you now.

Express and

Share your Love in all that you are and all that you do.

Make choices from your heart and remind

Yourself to

Stay in the present moment.

Other people are living their own dream and

Using their unique talents and gifts.

Letting yourself be

Who you are

And

Not comparing yourself to others allows your natural

Talents and gifts

To be

Offered more easily without

Expecting yourself to be "good enough."

Xpressing from your heart instead of

People pleasing allows you to experience and share the

Rich

Expression of your

Spirit and your Authentic

Self expression.

WHAT DOES MY SOUL WANT TO BRING TO THE WORLD?

What do I
Have to offer?
A lot of Wisdom and Love.
Today you can
Decide to
Offer what comes natural for you and
Express your Love with everyone you
See,
Making a difference in
Your life and the world. Your
Soul is creating
Opportunities for you now and
Using you to express
Love in the
World. Let go of any
Attachments to a role or identity and
Notice the yearnings from your soul
That guide you.
Today,
Offer yourself a way to
Believe in yourself, trust and let yourself
Reveal the wisdom and love that wants to flow through you.
In letting it flow easily and
Naturally you'll find yourself
Going into
Territory that will
Offer you
The experience you are
Here to have,
Experiences that
Will
Open new doors to a
Rich and rewarding
Life as you allow the
Desires of your soul to guide you.

YEARNING OF YOUR SOUL

Yearnings are cravings from your soul.

Everyone of us has had cravings or dreams

At one time or another.

Remember these cravings and bring them into the

Now, the present moment. Follow your

Intuitive yearning to find your true calling.

Notice the feelings that arise as you

Give thoughts to your dreams.

Open yourself and expand your comfort zone.

Fantasize about what

You want to create and

Open yourself to the

Understanding of your soul,

Reach for the stars and take a

Step today in that direction and you will soon find

Opportunities begin to present themselves from

Unknown places. Take some time today and

Listen to your soul.

WHAT DOES MY SOUL HAVE TO SAY?

What your soul
Has to say is to be
Aware of
The things that you
Desire. Your desires are
Offering you the
Experience your
Soul wants to have,
Meaning;
Your
Soul is
Offering you
Understanding of the
Life you want to
Have by giving you
A
Vision. It's
Expressing
To you the
Opportunities for you to
See what you truly want through the
Awareness of what
You desire.

HOW CAN I BE PRODUCTIVE TODAY?

Here is an

Opportunity

Where you

Can

Allow yourself to

Notice what needs to be changed

In what you

Believe; where you made agreements in the past.

Every

Personal belief

Reveals an agreement that you made which

Offered you some kind of fulfillment at the time.

Decide today to

Understand how you

Create

The circumstances

In your life; what beliefs are creating your situations?

Value this time as an opportunity to create new

Experiences and beliefs.

Today is an

Opportunity for you to

Decide to

Allow yourself to change

Your life by changing your thoughts and beliefs.

WHERE DO I BELONG?

Where you belong is right
Here, right now. When you are
Experiencing
Resistance it brings you out of the
Experience of belonging.
Doing things
Or finding a place
In which you "Need" to
Belong blocks your true
Experience of belonging.
Living fully in your body
Offers you your
Natural belonging and will
Give you true fulfillment.

HOW CAN I FEEL MORE CONNECTED TO OTHERS?

Having the feeling
Of connecting to others comes
When you are able to
Connect with yourself. Your outer world is
A reflection of your inner world. What's
Necessary
Is to notice the ways in which you've disconnected
From yourself and allow yourself to
Experience a re-connection.
Experience what it would be
Like now; take a deep breath and close your eyes,
Move into your heart and love and embrace all of you right now. This
Offers you a
Re-connection from within and the
Experience of
Connecting with yourself will create
Opportunities to
Naturally connect with others.
Notice where inside you need love and allow the love from your heart to
Expand throughout your entire being.
Connecting with others starts from within.
Today you have the opportunity to
Experience love from the inside and by
Doing this you're creating an intimacy within
That moves you into intimacy with
Others. Right now is a beautiful
Opportunity to LOVE all of you.
Today you are moving into
Having a new connection with yourself through the
Experience of love and as you experience love you
Radiate the vibration of love attracting other
Souls into the experience with you.

HOW CAN I RELEASE THE NEED FOR RECOGNITION?

Here is an
Opportunity
Where you
Can
Allow
New
Insights. Needing
Recognition comes from
Expressing fear.
Love is the
Experience that
Allows you to
See
Everyone and everything
Through the eyes of
Honor.
Every time you
Need to
Experience recognition the
Experience
Doesn't
Fulfill you because you're
Offering to get
Recognition.
Realize that
Everything in
Creation is an
Offering of
Greatness. Honoring your
Natural expression
Is all
That
Is necessary. By honoring yourself you are
Opening to a
Natural recognition from nature.

WHAT IS THE REST OF MY LIFE ABOUT?

What you
Hope for right now isn't
Always the
Thing you ultimately want.
If you want to
See what your life will be about,
Turn within and notice what's
Happening inside, what you're thinking now is creating your
Experiences. Letting go of
Resistance and judgments will help you to
Experience new
Situations, better than you can imagine right now.
Today is all you have, stay in the present moment and notice if
Old patterns keep showing up that no longer serve you.
Forgive yourself and others and update your beliefs as you
Move forward in a more positive direction. When
You forgive,
Let go and trust
It allows the
Flow to guide you into new
Experiences.
Are you ready to
Believe in yourself and what you have to
Offer? If you are then
Ultimately your experiences will reveal
The truth of what your life is about.

IS THERE ANYTHING I NEED TO KNOW ABOUT MY PATH?

It is
Simple;
The path is
Here, it's this
Experience
Right now. This
Experience is
All there is.
Notice how
You project into
The future and come back to the
Here and now.
In this moment what you
Need is being
Given to you.
It is important to
Notice how you
Experience the moment, see if you
Expect things to be
Different then what
They are. All of life is filled with wonderful
Opportunities and experiences.
Keep coming back to the
Now, this is where you
Obtain the
Wisdom and
Awareness of what you
Believe.
Out of
Understanding
The beliefs you have, it will assist you in creating new
Meanings if
You choose. This is your
Part in
Arranging
The life you intend to
Have.

WHAT IS THE RESISTANCE ABOUT?

Why you are
Having resistance is that you have
A competing part of you
That
Is
Scared because it feels
That if you share your creativity you
Have to have it perfect and it doesn't feel that it's perfect
Enough so it's creating the
Resistance. It's
Expressing resistance as a way to
Say to you that
It feels pressured by you, that if it creates it must be
Successful and receive recognition from others in order
To share.
Allowing yourself to
Notice this is giving you the opportunity to choose to
Create for the joy of creating.
Express to the part of you that feels pressured that you
Are now allowing it to create
Because it feels good and
Offer it/you Love and Acceptance and allow the
Universe to bring forth what is necessary as you continue
To create for the love and joy of being a channel for God.

HOW CAN I RELEASE THE RESISTANCE?

Have this moment be an

Opportunity

Where you

Celebrate

All that's in your life right

Now.

Imagine

Releasing the resistance and

Experiencing gratitude for

Life. The

Experience of gratitude offers you

A way that

Says your life

Experience is valuable.

This is

How to

Experience a

Release from resistance.

Every thought of gratitude

Says that you are thankful,

It unlocks the key of positive energy.

Saying

Thank you brings forth the

Awareness of enough and more.

Noticing this

Creates a way for you to

Experience how blessed you are.

IS THERE ANYTHING I NEED TO KNOW?

It's important for you to
See
That all of your experiences
Have significance.
Every experience you are having
Right now are
Experiences that
Are appropriate for you,
Notice that they are assisting you in your process.
You are
Trying too
Hard sweetie; let go,
It's
Not necessary to
Get somewhere now,
It is more
Necessary for you to
Experience what you need to
Experience, there is an integration taking place.
Decide
Today that you will
Offer yourself
Kindness as you allow yourself to
Notice what's
Occurring in your unconscious. Relax sweetie, everything
Will be okay, everything is okay, You Are Loved!

WHAT IS THIS ANGER TELLING ME?

What's
Happening is you
Are becoming aware of
The ways
In which you
Sabotage
The things you want to
Have. The anger
Is
Showing you that you
Are ready
Now to
Go with what you're
Expressing. It's
Revealing to you
That you are
Experiencing internal betrayal.
Let it speak
Let it tell you it's positive purpose.
It's helping you
Notice that you can't
Get away with the promises you
Mention to yourself without allowing yourself to
Experience them, it wants you to have all that you desire.

WHAT IS TRUE ABOUT MY LIFE?

What's

Happening is you

Are finding

Truth inside yourself and

In this truth you can't

Stay

The same.

Right now you're beginning to

Understand that your

Experiences

Are

Brought about as

Opportunities for you to

Understand

Truth by

Making

Your

Life about your

Internal guidance and

Following it as you continue to

Explore new avenues.

HOW CAN I EMBRACE MY POWER FEARLESS?

Here is an
Opportunity
Where you
Can
Allow
New experiences
In without
Expecting anything or
Making what you
Believed in the past to be
Right today.
All of
Creation is an
Experience of
Moving.
You are in the
Process of
Opening to and following the
Will of the divine.
Even though you might have
Resistance, you don't have to Stay there. Being
Fearless is the
Experience of being
Able to
Release the idea of being a victim and
Letting your natural
Expression
Shine as you
Stay true to your heart and soul.

ARE THERE ANY FEARS BLOCKING ME TODAY?

As you allow more of yourself to be
Revealed you're starting to
Experience
The fears that you
Had about
Expressing yourself.
Right now what you are
Experiencing is
A way that your
Natural self is guiding
You and you are walking through the
Fear you had in the past about
Expressing
Authentically and
Revealing your true self.
See the
Belief you had about yourself and
Life that
Offered you a fear about what you
Could or couldn't express.
Keep
In mind that your
Needs are
Giving you clues to the
Meaning you put on your
Experiences.
The need for protection, safety and fear of
Others offers you a way that you
Don't allow yourself the freedom of expression. Today,
Allow yourself to take your attention off fear and place
Your attention on LOVE and the freedom of expressing your true self.

WHY AM I FEELING DISORIENTED?

What's

Happening is

You

Are

Moving from the known to the unknown, from

Insight into

Following the insight into a new

Experience. The

Experience of feeling disoriented is

Letting you know that you are

In an experience that's not yet familiar for you.

Nature is

Giving you this opportunity to

Design your life

In a new way. This

Situation is being

Offered to

Release what

Is known so that you can

Experience a more fulfilling life

Now.

The disorientation you are

Experiencing is removing what

Doesn't serve you and allowing you to experience truth.

HOW CAN I FUNCTION FROM MY INNER MOST CENTER?

Here is an
Opportunity
Where you
Can
Awaken into
New territory.
If you let
Fear guide you it's
Useless.
Now is the time to
Create and
Trust
In what you have to
Offer the world. It's
Necessary
For you to
Remember your
Oneness with the
Magnificence of your creator as you
Move through
Your life.
In
Noticing your
Natural ways of
Expressing, you're allowing your true self to
Reveal itself
More and more.
Out of this you'll be able to
Share from and experience
The truth inside you.
Creating from this space allows your
Experiences to flow more easily and
Naturally and you'll be coming from
The space of your natural
Expression, the
Real you, the internal you.

WHAT DOES IT MEAN TO REVEAL MYSELF?

When you are revealing yourself you're
Honoring
All
That you are, you're
Dancing to the rhythm of your heart and
Offering your Authentic
Expression
Sincerely.
It's letting go of
The excuses or beliefs you
Made in the past of why you couldn't
Express and you're
Allowing your
Natural self
To shine. Revealing yourself is
Offering the
Richness of your authentic
Expression, allowing yourself to be
Vulnerable and letting your natural
Expression be seen
And heard. Revealing yourself is
Letting your true
Magnificence out, it's allowing
Your authentic
Self
Expression to
Lead, guide and direct your life,
Fulfilling your divine purpose.

WHAT IS DIVINE SUCCESS?

When you are
Having divine success you
Are allowing yourself
To experience the Joy
In being alive. Divine
Success is
Doing what you Love and Loving what you do,
It's
Valuing your life experience
In ways that you're allowing your
Natural
Essence to be expressed. Divine
Success is
Understanding your
Connection with your
Creator, it's the
Experience of
Seeing through the eyes of
Source.

WHAT DOES IT MEAN TO BE HEALED?

What do I
Have to do to heal?
Are you looking for something
To
Do? It's more about
Offering yourself love in all of your
Experiences. It's
Staying
In
The present
Moment and allowing whatever you're
Experiencing to be okay. In loving and
Appreciating yourself and your experiences you will
Notice a healing
Taking place and you'll have the
Opportunity to
Believe and trust that
Everything is working for your
Highest good and that all of your
Experiences are serving you in one way or
Another. When you
Love yourself
Everyone and everything this is
Divine healing.

HOW CAN I ENHANCE MY SELF ESTEEM?

Here you can
Offer a belief in
Who you are and
Care
About yourself and your
Needs
In all your
Experiences. When you have
Needs and you
Have the
Ability to
Naturally
Care about yourself, you are
Experiencing value and
Meaning in
Yourself.
Self
Esteem is
Love
For yourself, it is the
Experience that
Says you
Trust your creator and your natural
Expression. It's the
Experience of believing that your true self has
Meaning and purpose.

HOW CAN I LIVE FROM MY FEMININE NATURE?

Here you are doing so right now. You are
Open and
Willing to receive divine guidance.
Coming from
A space of receptivity is a
Natural way that allows
In the
Love and guidance of the divine and opens you to your
Intuition. When you are
Valuing the
Experience you'll
Find nature
Revealing and
Offering you
More,
Meaning; when
You are open and receptive you'll
Find that your
Experiences have
More meaning because you are following your
Intuition; your true
Nature.
It's
Natural to
Experience love, intuition and guidance from the divine, this is your
Natural state.
Allowing yourself
To
Understand what's
Real allows you to
Experience truth more fully.

HOW CAN I FOCUS MY ENERGY NOW?

Have

Options

Where you

Can see

Abundance. Allow yourself to

Naturally become aware of ways

In which you can

Find

Opportunities to

Create new ideas.

Understand that

Seeing options helps you to

Move in a new direction. When

You

Expand your awareness you invite

New ideas, new possibilities, new

Experiences into your life.

Right now you can

Give

Your energy to

Noticing new

Options, new ideas that

Will bring you greater fulfillment and joy.

HOW CAN I ACCEPT AND ENJOY MY LIFE NOW?

Have an
Offering of abundance
Where you've seen scarcity in the past,
Creation itself can bring joy.
A feeling of enjoyment comes
Naturally when you are
In the flow and
Allowing
Creation to happen easily and naturally.
Control and
Expectations often create blocks, allow yourself to be a
Participant; a co-creator with the universe.
Today, give yourself permission to
Allow things to unfold
Naturally.
Decide to view all of your
Experiences as
Necessary.
Joy comes from acceptance,
Opening to your
Your natural gifts and allowing them to
Move through
You to into the world.
Life
Is more joyful when you are
Flowing with your
Experiences easily and
Naturally. Let go sweetie, you are being
Offered something
Wonderful, it's safe to let go and live in the flow.

HOW CAN I LIVE IN BALANCE TODAY?

Having balance is
Obtaining a
Way where you
Can
Allow your
Natural
Instincts to guide your
Life.
It's when you are
Valuing all of your life
Experiences and allowing yourself to
Include taking care of your own
Needs; physical, mental, emotional and spiritual.
Balance is
Aligning yourself with God's
Love for you and
Allowing your
Natural self to be the
Creator of your life.
Everything
That is being
Offered from your connection to the
Divine is
A way for
You to live in balance.

WHAT DO YOU WANT TO DO TODAY?

What about

Having

A celebration

Today to honor your

Divinity!

Offer gratitude for

Your life experience and the

Opportunity to

Understand and experience divine love. Take a

Walk in nature

And

Notice and appreciate

The natural beauty that's all around you.

Thank god for this

Opportunity to be alive.

Deciding to

Offer

This celebration of and for life allows you to

Open more to your

Divine nature

And to experience the beauty, joy and love that's in

You, through you and all around you.

HOW DO YOU WANT ME TO SHOW UP TODAY?

Have an
Openness to
Whatever is happening and allow the
Divine to
Offer
You what you need. Stay
Open and
Understand that
What you want
And what you
Need might be different.
Trust and surrender as you
Move into your
Experiences
Today. You have this
Opportunity now to
Start a new way of
Honoring yourself and life by being
Open to the notion that
Whatever is happening is helping you to
Understand your infinite
Potential.
Trust life to bring you
Opportunities in
Divine order and that
All is serving
Your higher purpose.

HOW CAN MY HEART REACH OTHER HEARTS?

Having your heart
Open is
What you
Can do. When you
Are
Noticing the
Movement in
Your
Heart wanting to
Express and experience love, you
Are
Reaching into
The hearts of others.
Right now by
Experiencing love, you
Are
Creating an opening in your
Heart and
Other hearts feel
This and
Have the
Experience too.
Receive the gift of love from the
Heavens above and allow this
Experience of love to radiate from you and
All around you and your heart will be
Reaching
The hearts and
Souls of all beings on earth.

WHAT NEW DIRECTION AM I FACING?

What's
Happening is you
Are
Taking a
New route. It's time to
Express
What you have inside, your
Divine nature.
If you
Resist your
Experiences you
Cannot
Take
In all that the universe is
Offering you
Now.
All that is happening now is
Moving you
In a new direction,
Flow with it sweetie
And see where it takes you, have the
Courage to
Invite the
New, open your heart and
Give yourself a chance.

WHY DO I FEAR THE WORD NEW?

Why you

Have a fear of the word new is that

You've

Decided that new experiences will

Offer you disappointment or failure based on

Instances and perceptions from past experiences.

Facing all your

Experiences now with a knowing that all is divine will

Allow you to move through the

Resistance you had in the past.

Today and everyday is an opportunity to

Have new experiences. Notice what belief is being

Expressed through your actions. Do you feel

Worthy of having new or wonderful

Opportunities? Notice what's being

Revealed by the way you are choosing to live.

Decide today that it's okay for you to have

New and wonderful

Experiences, that you are worth it, you are

Worthy of it, you are supported and YOU ARE LOVED!

HOW CAN I EMBRACE LIFE MORE FULLY?

Here is an

Opportunity

Where you

Can

Achieve all that is

Natural for you.

In this moment

Experience what it's like to be part of the

Magnificence of creation itself.

Bring to your awareness the idea that you're

Right where you need to be

And you're learning what you

Came here to learn. Your

Experiences in

Life are the experiences

In which are perfectly designed

For you.

Explore what it

Means to

Open to the magnificence and

Richness of your authentic

Expression,

Feel what it's like to

Use your natural way of

Living be the way you now

Let

Yourself embrace your life more fully.

HELP ME TO RELEASE JEALOUSY

Having the

Experience of jealousy

Lets you

Prepare to

Move into the

Experience that you want

To have for yourself.

Other people are

Revealing to you an

Experience that's possible for you in your

Life

Experience.

As you continue to

State to the universe the

Experiences you want to have from a place of

Joy, and you take steps in that direction, soon you'll

Experience that or something better in your own life.

As you see the things you want in your

Life in the

Outer, it's an opportunity for you to

Use that experience to

See that it's also possible for

You so CELEBRATE IT!

WHAT'S TRYING TO GET MY ATTENTION?

What's

Happening is that you are now willing to have

All

That you

Say you want

To have so

Right now

You are

In situations that are activating what

Needs to be healed in order for you to

Generate new opportunities.

The unresolved issues that are being

Offered in your situations are

Giving you the opportunity to bring them into the light. The

Experiences you are having now are bringing up

The issues that are ready to be healed,

Meaning,

You're being

Activated from

The inside; can you see

This as a blessing? All of your

Experiences are here to assist you in becoming your

Natural self.

Today you are

In a time

Of becoming whole, you're creating a

New sense of self-love, freedom and inner peace.

HOW DO I FIND MYSELF? THIS IS ME?

Here you are and
Out of being right here, right now is
Where you find
Debra. She's not
Outside, she's
In you.
Finding yourself is
Inside you, it's your
Natural
Divinity, it's what
Moves
You. Close your eyes and
Sense and
Experience what it's
Like to
Feel your essence from within.

The experience that you're
Having right now
Is you, your
Sacred self. Really notice how
It feels,
Sense yourself from within and
Move with your natural
Expression. Congratulations, you found yourself.

WHAT IS THE RICHNESS OF WHO I AM?

What you
Have is
A genuine way
To be
In the world. Your
Spirit is
The light and
Honor of your
Expression. Your
Richness
Is your
Creativity that
Honors your
Natural
Expression, your authentic
Self.
Surrender and
Open yourself to the
Flow and
Watch
How
Opportunities come
Into your life that
Are in alignment with your natural
Magnificence.

WHAT'S HAPPENING HERE?

What's

Happening here is

Asking you

To

See that you are

Having some internal conflict

And it's creating fear and resistance. There are

Parts of you that are still in the

Past and haven't resolved certain issues from past

Experiences. This is showing you what

Needs forgiveness so you can be

Integrated into the fullness of your true self. It's

Necessary for you to

Get all parts of you in

Harmony in order for you to easily and naturally

Experience what you're now

Ready to

Experience in your life.

I'M NOT SURE WHAT I'M AFRAID OF?

It's okay not to
Make any decisions right
Now. Today is an
Opportunity
To understand your
Spirit.
Understanding your spirit
Reveals the
Experience in
Which you truly want to
Have.
Allow
This time to be a time of
Inspiration.
Moving in
A direction will
Flow naturally when you're
Ready.
All
Is in
Divine
Order. Everything is going to be okay sweetie, let go of
Fear and emerce yourself in unconditional love.

WHAT'S BEING EXPRESSED FROM SPIRIT?

What's
Happening is you
Are being
Taken into
Surrender
Because controlling your
Experiences hasn't worked
In the past and
Now you're being
Given an opportunity to
Experience the
Xperience of surrender,
Patience and trust.
Right now this
Experience is
Showing you that when you
Surrender you have the opportunity to
Experience and trust in the
Divine. The
Feeling of trust allows
Resistance to fall away and lets new
Opportunities show up that are
More in alignment with your true
Self. By surrendering your will and being open, receptive and
Present you have the opportunity to hear your
Intuition
Revealing your
Internal
Truth.

WHAT WANTS TO BE EXPRESSED?

When you
Have
An idea
That inspires you, it
Wants to be expressed.
Allow yourself to
Notice
That expressing is also
Surrendering
The
Outcome.
Being in surrender allows the
Experience to do what it needs to without
Expectations. Give yourself the
Xperience and
Pleasure of
Radiating and
Expressing
Sincerely while
Surrendering any
Expectations or outcome to the
Divine.

WHAT DOES IT MEAN TO BE COMPETENT?

When you
Have competence you
Are in a space of
Trusting your
Divine nature. Feeling competent
Offers you the
Experience of
Strength. Being competent
Is believing in yourself and all
That you are;
Meaning, the
Experience of believing in yourself
Activates feelings of capability and your
Natural strengths.
Today is an
Opportunity to
Become the
Experience of a
Competent person by
Opening yourself to
More
Possibilities, believing in yourself,
Expressing your
Truth and
Exploring and sharing your
Natural
Talents and gifts.

WHAT'S A LOVING DECISION I CAN MAKE?

What you
Have already is
A natural way of
Taking
Situations
And being able to
Let them be
Opportunities of a
Valuable experience.
It's noticing this that
Gives you
Divine power, divine love. Your
Experiences are
Created by what you believe
Inside.
State your
Intention to be
Offered
New
Insights on
Creating
A
Naturally loving life;
Meaning,
Ask for the most
Kindest and loving ways to
Experience Love for yourself and all of humanity.

WHAT IS A FULL LIFE EXPERIENCE?

When you
Have
A life of
Trust
In
Spirit
And you personally
Fulfill your own needs. When you
Use
Life to
Love all that
Life brings you
In the moment and you
Find
Each
Experience to be an
Xperience of
Pleasure, an
Experience of the
Richness of being alive and
In the moment. When you allow every
Experience to be a
Necessary part of
Creation and you allow your authentic
Expression to shine.

HOW CAN I EXPERIENCE LIFE MORE?

Have
Options
Where you
Can
Allow yourself to do
New things.
It's when you are open to
Experiencing more, that more can come into your
Xperiences. When you make a commitment to
Participate in and
Experience life more, it allows more to be
Revealed.
In making a commitment to what you want to
Experience, you're telling the universe that you're ready.
Notice what you want and
Create ways to bring these opportunities into your life
Experience.
Life
Is here
For you, it wants you to
Enjoy it.
Make it a priority everyday to be
Open and
Receptive to
Experiencing life more fully.

WHAT DOES IT MEAN TO BE WORTHY?

What it means to be worthy is

Honoring

All

That you are. Your

Divine nature is the

Offering of your worth. Your

Experience here on earth

Says you are worthy. You are made

In

The image of god and this

Makes you worthy. Your natural

Expression is

All you

Need

To feel worthy. Your worth doesn't come from the

Outside or doing something to

Be worthy. Your worth is your

Essence, you are

Worthy because of who you are. Today is an

Opportunity to

Remind you

That you are worthy, you don't

Have to prove it by doing more, getting more etc.

You are worthy because you are you!

WHAT IS MY DIVINE NATURE?

When you are
Having peace inside
And you are
Trusting that everything
Is serving a higher purpose.
Surrendering the need to control as you
Move through
Your experiences will help you connect to your
Divine nature.
Intend each day for a
Vision of love and
Invite this vision to flow through you to everyone.
Nature has a way of
Expressing itself as you stay open to the
Newness of each moment
And begin
To allow a deeper
Understanding of the love and
Richness of who you are to become your
Expression.

HOW CAN I SURRENDER TO THE DIVINE?

Here is an
Opportunity
Where you
Can become more
Aware of what
Naturally
Is being
Shown to you, a way to
Use your energy
Right now.
Rather than
Expecting what
Needs to happen,
Decide now that you will allow
Every experience to be
Right for you.
Today,
Offer
Trust in the moment and the
How will be shown to you.
Expressing that you trust allows the
Divine to give you an
Internal
Vision that
Is more in alignment with your
Natural
Expression.

WHAT IS GODS WILL FOR MY LIFE?

What Gods will for you is that you experience

Happiness, peace and love in all that you

Are and all

That you do.

Inspiration is

Showing you

Gods will and

Offering you your

Desires.

See

What

Inspires you and

Let it into your

Life. Take a deep breath and

Fill every cell and fiber of your being with LOVE.

Offering yourself love is

Revealing gods will

Moving through

You.

Love, peace, joy and happiness

Is what god wants

For your life

Experience.

WHAT DOES GODS LOVE FEEL LIKE?

When you
Have an internal peace
About all
That's happening. Feeling
Divine love, gods love,
Offers you the
Experience of being
Special, cared for, it
Generates the
Offering of love.
Divine love
Shares
Love with yourself and
Others
Vulnerably and the
Experience
Feels like
Eternal bliss,
Eternal freedom. Gods
Love
Lives in you
In your heart and soul, it's your inner
Knowing, your true
Expression.

WHAT ARE THE SIGNS I'M RECEIVING?

What's
Happening is you
Are in a
Time of re-
Arranging. You're
Ready to
Experience all
That you
Have been saying you want to
Experience.
Stay
In the flow by
Giving
Nature your
Surrender. What you need will be given to you
In the right, perfect
Moment.
Realize that all of your
Experiences are important and they have a
Certain lesson or blessing to
Experience.
In
Valuing every experience now
It lets you be in
Natural harmony with the universe, allowing in the
Gifts of learning, healing, experiencing love and miracles.

BEAUTIFUL SPIRIT

Beauty is in you, through you and
Everywhere. Beauty is
All that is.
Understanding
This allows you to be
In tune with the
Fulfillment of nature.
Understanding real
Love and beauty is noticing the
Spirit of love that you are,
Perfect as the
Intelligence that created you. You are a
Radiant light of LOVE,
Intelligent, wise, loving and compassionate.
This is who you are a Beautiful Spirit.

WHAT IS THIS FEELING OF LOVE?

What's
Happening is you
Are feeling your
True essence, your
Internal world is
Sensing
The energy of the divine.
Having this moment
Is
Showing you the
Feeling and
Experience of your true
Essence, which is
Love. Your
Innate
Nature is
Giving you the
Offering and
Feeling of being
Loved. Be
Open to the
Value of this
Experience, this is your natural state of being.

LIFE IS A BEAUTIFUL GIFT

Life
Is a beautiful gift of ever
Flowing wonderful
Experiences, new
Inventions and
Sharing love.
All of gods creations are
Beautifully and uniquely designed,
Everything in life is
A gift.
Using your natural
Talents and gifts
Is the gift of gods energy
Flowing through you,
Using you as a channel for inspiration and
Love.
Giving and receiving love
Is a gift that is constantly
Flowing in you,
Through you and all around you.

WHAT IS MY SOUL'S PURPOSE?

When you
Have a question of your soul's purpose you are
Asking
To reveal your
Internal expression, your
Soul is the
Magnificence of who
You truly are.
Staying true to your heart
Opens you to your divinity and you
Understand what it's like to
Love yourself and others unconditionally. Your
Soul's purpose is to lead, guide and direct your life and
Provide for you all you need when you need it.
Understanding and experiencing the
Richness and the
Purpose of your soul allows your heart to
Open as you
Share your wisdom and compassion and
Express LOVE to all.

WHAT IS MY SOUL CREATING FOR ME TODAY?

What's
Happening is
A way
That your soul
Is
Saying that it's ready to share its
Magnificence.
Your
Soul is
Offering you a way to
Use your
Life as a
Co-creator.
Realize that the
Experiences that
Are in your life right now are
Taking you
Into
New territory and allowing you to
Give
From the space
Of your
Real self, your true
Magnificence. As you
Experience your true magnificence
The vibration will bring forth
Opportunities that are part of your
Divine plan
And the fulfillment of
Your soul.

WHAT IS JOY OF THE SOUL?

When you are
Having
A feeling
That
Is
So amazing, you're filled with so much
Joy and love and you're
Open and free flowing. When
You are
Offering your love with everyone and everything,
Feeling free,
Trusting and
Honorable and your
Expressing yourself
Sincerely, feeling that all that's
Occurring in life is an
Ultimate experience of
LOVE.

HOW HAVE I TRANSFORMED?

How you've transformed is you've
Opened to
What you've
Had
As a
Vision, the
Experience
In which your
True self is now a
Reality. You
Are easily and
Naturally
Sharing from the
Fullness
Of your
Real self; your true
Magnificence and you're
Experiencing unconditional love, your
Divine nature.

I AM FREE TO BE MY TRUE SELF

Ignite your passion, you
Are ready. You've
Made tremendous progress
From
Resistance to
Experiencing your divine
Essence. You are more
Trusting and
Open and have
Become self
Empowered,
More
Your
True self.
Right now is the opportunity to
Use your personal
Experience to
Share with others how you've come to
Experience true
Love and trust
From within.

Suggestions on Listening to Your Inner Wisdom

Find a quiet place where you can be alone and undisturbed, a place that brings you feelings of peace and tranquility. If you don't have one, you now have an opportunity to create it. Place any symbols, pictures, cards, flowers, play soft music or anything that brings you good feelings and a connection to the divine.

Have a pen and a lot of paper in front of you. Sitting at a table or desk is advisable; however, it's not necessary. When you're ready close your eyes and become aware of your breathing, notice your breath moving easily and naturally in and out of your body, feeling more and more relaxed with each and every breath.

You might want to consider calling forth the presence, love, protection and guidance of god, angels and all the divine beings who work with you and ask that any negativity, judgments, misunderstandings, fears, doubts or worries that may be present in your consciousness be cleared and lifted to the highest realms of light and sound where it may be transformed and used in service for the highest good for all concerned and ask to be filled with light and love and surrounded by grace.

Take a moment to talk to your guides about your issue and ask only what's in your highest good to be brought forth and then set your intention. For example; "My intention is to resolve this issue with…" or "My intention is to be more accepting" or "My intention is to receive guidance or clarity" or "My intention is to open my heart and experience Love" or "My intention is to be happy and at peace."

When you are ready, open your eyes, you might feel a little drowsy and that's okay, in fact it's better. With your non dominant hand write your question along the edge of the paper going down; you can see the example in my book. Go back to the top of the page and look at the first letter and write the first word that comes to you. Relax beyond the intellect of the mind into a deeper place from within and allow the energy to guide your pen; and keep breathing. Do your best not to read what you've written until you've completed writing. If you get stuck, close your eyes and focus on your breathing again and when you are ready, open your eyes and continue from where you paused. When you're done, read what came forth. Sometimes you'll get the answers or guidance with one process or you might be given the opportunity to do another process or be guided to do something else. For example: I'm often guided to talk (gestalt) with whatever I'm having an issue with or I'll be guided to forgive and I'll be given a new perception or sometimes I'm guided to just trust and surrender into the loving. There are infinite possibilities that come forth. Trust that whatever comes forth is right for you at the time and remember, the divine only shares positive, constructive and loving guidance. Do your best to stay with the process until you feel a positive internal shift. When you're done, breathe in the love from source and create a positive affirmation, write it down, meditate on it and repeat it often throughout the day and as you're drifting off to sleep at night.

Sometimes the information you receive doesn't seem logical or make sense and the answers might seem irrelevant to the question you're asking, however it might be exactly what you need. Often I will start my day with "Is there anything that I need to know?" Remember to keep an open mind, allow your awareness to expand and give yourself the opportunity and gift of listening to your inner wisdom, you'll be amazed of the wonderful insight, knowledge and LOVE that's inside you. May you find this process to be fun, uplifting, empowering, inspiring and healing.

My Bio

Debra Mittler is a warm and compassionate healer with a unique ability to touch people's hearts and souls. She has a deep passion for spiritual growth and enjoys assisting others in developing and cultivating nurturing and loving ways of being with themselves, others and following their heartfelt dreams.

Diagnosed with anorexia nervosa at age 13, and spending a quarter of a century going in and out of hospitals and treatment centers, Debra experienced first hand what it was like living with the degradation of an eating disorder and self hatred. Through her own healing she's been able to go beneath the symptom and discover self love, personal power, strength, wisdom and inner peace.

Debra is a leading authority in overcoming obstacles and supports her clients by holding a space of unconditional love and offering encouragement, effective tools and valuable insights allowing them to experience and listen to their own inner wisdom. Debra offers her clients the opportunity to experience the most precious gift in the world; a real genuine way to love, honor, value and appreciate themselves, others and their life experience.

Debra is a graduate of the Master's Program in Spiritual Psychology from the University of Santa Monica and A graduate of Hypnosis Motivation Institute.

Debra is available for one-on-one sessions, speaking engagements and facilitating workshops.

For more information you can contact Debra Mittler at (310) 948-9997

DEBRA@LIVINGINTHELOVING.COM
WWW.LIVINGINTHELOVING.COM
HTTP://POETICHEALING.WORDPRESS.COM

Made in the USA
Las Vegas, NV
03 March 2023